SERIAL MURDER 101

SERIAL MURDER | 101

BRIDGET DiCOSMO

BERKLEY BOOKS, NEW YORK

THE BERKLEY PUBLISHING GROUP
Published by the Penguin Group
Penguin Group (USA) Inc.
375 Hudson Street, New York, New York 10014, USA
Penguin Group (Canada), 90 Eglinton Avenue East, Suite 700, Toronto, Ontario M4P 2Y3, Canada
(a division of Pearson Penguin Canada Inc.)
Penguin Books Ltd., 80 Strand, London WC2R 0RL, England
Penguin Group Ireland, 25 St. Stephen's Green, Dublin 2, Ireland (a division of Penguin Books Ltd.)
Penguin Group (Australia), 250 Camberwell Road, Camberwell, Victoria 3124, Australia
(a division of Pearson Australia Group Pty. Ltd.)
Penguin Books India Pvt. Ltd., 11 Community Centre, Panchsheel Park, New Delhi—110 017, India
Penguin Group (NZ), 67 Apollo Drive, Rosedale, North Shore 0632, New Zealand
(a division of Pearson New Zealand Ltd.)
Penguin Books (South Africa) (Pty.) Ltd., 24 Sturdee Avenue, Rosebank, Johannesburg 2196,
South Africa

Penguin Books Ltd., Registered Offices: 80 Strand, London WC2R 0RL, England

The publisher does not have any control over and does not assume any responsibility for author or
third-party websites or their content.

This is a true story. However, the names and identifying characteristics of certain people have been
changed to protect their privacy.

SERIAL MURDER 101

A Berkley Book / published by arrangement with the author

PRINTING HISTORY
Berkley mass-market edition / July 2009

Copyright © 2009 by Bridget DiCosmo
Cover design by Edwin Tse
Book design by Laura K. Corless

ISBN: 978-0-425-22698-8

BERKLEY®
Berkley Books are published by The Berkley Publishing Group,
a division of Penguin Group (USA) Inc.,
375 Hudson Street, New York, New York 10014.
BERKLEY is a registered trademark of Penguin Group (USA) Inc.
The "B" design is a trademark of Penguin Group (USA) Inc.

PRINTED IN THE UNITED STATES OF AMERICA

10   9   8   7   6   5   4   3   2   1

To the memory of the victims of these horrible murders, their families, and the detectives—past and present—who worked so hard on these cases; as well as to the victims and their families in every cold case, who wait so long for closure, which sometimes never comes.

Acknowledgments

I would like to thank the following agencies and individuals:

Bob Miller, Jon Rust, Cape Girardeau Police Department, Paul Echols, Jim Smith, Sam Blackwell, Cape Girardeau County Sheriff's Department, Cape Girardeau County Prosecuting Attorney's office, Bill Moushey, Berkley Books, Denise Silvestro, Steve Harris, Shannon Jamieson Vazquez, Meredith Giordan, Elizabeth Dodd, Peg McNichol, Sharon Sanders, Aaron Eisenhauer, Rudi Keller, Dustin Schoof, Amber Heimbach, Aunt Donna, Mom and Dad.

Prologue

The old man sat hunched over in the cramped visiting room of the Cape Girardeau County Jail, shoulders bunched together, skin nearly translucent against the neon orange of his jumpsuit.

He didn't look like a monster.

Salt-and-pepper hair cut close to a scalp that was prison-pale, deprived of sunlight for the past twenty-four years, Timothy Wayne Krajcir looked like a grandfather sitting in a nursing home hoping for a visit from his family. What he didn't resemble was a man facing a string of felony charges for some of the most brutal murders, rapes, and robberies in the history of Cape Girardeau, Missouri.

He peered at me through thick, black rubber glasses that had been issued to him since his move to the county jail from the maximum security facility in Tamms, Illinois.

Some prisons issue rubber frames to inmates with glasses so the pieces can't be broken and made into weapons. Krajcir wasn't happy about his latest eyewear, according to Detective Jimmy Smith. He was accustomed to thin, silver wire frames, and much preferred those. He had been relocated so he could be tried for five unsolved murders in Cape Girardeau. State law mandated he needed to be transferred to the custody of the county in which he was being charged.

Like Krajcir, Detective Smith had gray hair, but his was a more distinguished silver white. Smith sat stiffly in the folding chair at the head of the flat counsel table in the tiny, unadorned room. The visiting rooms at the county jail are little more than cells, far different from the brightly lit, spread-out areas, complete with vending machines, that the Missouri state prisons usually provide for inmates and their visitors.

In my time as crime reporter for Cape Girardeau's main newspaper, the *Southeast Missourian,* I had done several interviews with state inmates at the Missouri Department of Corrections, but never in Cape's county jail. John Jordan, longtime sheriff of Cape Girardeau County, usually didn't permit media interviews, but he'd made an exception today.

Krajcir's eyes were the most salient aspect of his appearance. Behind the glasses, they burned like dark holes in his ghostly face. Slight stubble dotted a rounded and fleshy jaw. He looked almost comical, the fuzzy gray buzz cut and thick black frames lending a caricature-type appeal to his face. His current gaunt physique did not hint at the athletic prowess I'd been told he'd once possessed: his former warden at the Illinois prison had described Krajcir as the best athlete he'd ever seen. Basketball was his game, as was baseball. In prison, he'd mostly associated with the other jocks. Sports had defined him during his time as an inmate.

The Timothy Krajcir I faced across the table was no longer that athlete. His body pitched forward slightly, sixty-three years of age showing in every line on his haggard face and in his slumped frame, still tall at over six feet, but now becoming frail and lacking definition. A combined thirty years spent in the Illinois prison system hadn't done him any favors. Shackles encased Krajcir's ankles and handcuffs bound his hands, rendering him helpless. Smith and a burly sheriff's deputy sat at the table anyway.

Krajcir had shown little interest in publicity up until this point. It was the third time I'd laid eyes on the man, and I still found it difficult to reconcile the slaughter wreaked upon the town of Cape Girardeau with the shriveled elderly gentleman who sat before me. His arrogance didn't match his looks. The conceited air struck me immediately. It was the attitude of someone who sincerely believed he possessed an intellect superior to everyone else's in the room.

Krajcir had already been safely behind bars in an Illinois state prison, serving the remainder of a sentence for child molestation after violating his parole in 1983. The homicides, five in Cape Girardeau, and four more in other cities, had occurred from 1977 to 1982. Krajcir had held his tongue for over two decades, only to confess once police used DNA to link him to one of the murders.

In the state of Missouri, the man faced five charges of capital murder, seven counts of sexual assault, and one armed robbery charge. Practically every killing contained some element—kidnapping, brutality, lying in wait—necessary to constitute a capital offense. Krajcir was guilty of all three elements in some, if not all, of the murders he was charged with. The sexual assaults that accompanied the murders more than satisfied the issue of brutality. He'd also kidnapped his victims, twice crossing state lines, had broken into their houses, and lain in wait for their return.

The slew of heinous offenses would've been enough to guarantee a death sentence in Missouri under normal circumstances, but without Krajcir's cooperation, these cases would never have come to conclusion. Rape victims and family members of those whom Krajcir had killed would never know the identity of the person responsible for destroying their lives. Without Krajcir's willingness to confess, he would've merely remained a potential suspect in the most terrifying murders ever committed in Cape Girardeau, just added to lists of hundreds of other suspects who'd had motive, opportunity, or were just plain oddballs from nearby neighborhoods. The fact was, the police needed Krajcir's confessions to secure a conviction. That had been enough to stay the man's execution.

In December 2007, Krajcir pleaded guilty to the 1982 killing of pretty, bright Deborah Sheppard, a coed found dead in her apartment a few blocks off the campus of Southern Illinois University, the same school Krajcir had attended. Sheppard's murder was the crime that had ultimately unraveled the string of homicides for police, when DNA evidence was discovered incriminating Krajcir.

Carbondale, Illinois, police detective Lieutenant Paul Echols was the detective who'd solved the Deborah Sheppard case, when he matched DNA from Sheppard's apartment to Krajcir, whose genetic profile was in the national database of convicted felons. Echols had garnered a reputation for being successful with cold-case homicides when he solved the murder of Susan Schumake, who died in 1981, her body found on a walking trail of Southern Illinois University; the homicide had gone unsolved for twenty-three years before Echols got hold of the case. He used DNA obtained from cigarette butts to match the genetic profile of a suspect in the murder to samples found at the crime scene and preserved. He got a hit with Daniel Woloson, and after Woloson's conviction, the chief of the Carbondale Police Department turned Deborah Sheppard's case over to Echols in the hopes he'd have the same success. His hopes were fulfilled, and then some.

Attorneys and investigators knew before Krajcir's plea hearing that he was going to plead guilty to Sheppard's murder. They were counting on it. He'd given no indication that he would be uncooperative enough to enter a not guilty plea, forcing a trial. Krajcir knew that they had more than enough physical evidence to secure a conviction, even without his confession. Krajcir's plea hearing on December 10, 2007, occurred without fanfare. He quietly entered his plea of guilty, and received a forty-year sentence for the murder of Deborah Sheppard.

When that sentence was handed down by a Jackson

County, Illinois, circuit judge, three things were accomplished. One, Sheppard's parents finally received the much-needed closure they'd craved since the death of their daughter twenty-five years earlier. Two, the sentence ensured that Krajcir, already in his early sixties, would probably die in prison. Before pleading guilty to killing Sheppard, Krajcir technically could have decided to start working toward his own release, since he was only in prison on a civil commitment. What that amounted to was an agreement with the state of Illinois that he was a sexual predator who should not be allowed freedom unless he showed prison officials drastic improvement in his condition. But Krajcir had fooled officials into giving him parole before. Sexual predators have an extraordinarily high rate of recidivism, or reoffending, but prior to his previous release in 1981, Krajcir had attended counseling sessions and group therapy, and had participated in his own diagnosis to the point that therapists believed he was safe to release into the world again. When Krajcir was re-imprisoned in 1983, it was for having been found with a loaded gun—an automatic violation of his parole, since it's illegal for convicted felons to possess guns. After that, he stayed in prison, and eventually stopped trying to convince anyone he was fit for release. If he had chosen to participate in the sex offender programs offered by the prison, he very well might have been released again. Now, however, as a convicted murderer, he would not be seeing daylight for a long time.

The third thing the Illinois murder conviction did was lead Cape Girardeau County prosecutor Morley Swingle to charge Krajcir formally with the five murders and three rapes Krajcir had committed in Missouri. In deference to those working the Sheppard case, Swingle had held off on formally charging Krajcir until he'd received word that the Illinois plea hearing had been successful. Hours after Krajcir acknowledged his guilt in killing Sheppard, Swingle put a prepared warrant in front of a Missouri judge. The warrant charged Krajcir with the murders of five women, two of whom he'd also raped, as well as a third rape in which the victim hadn't been killed.

Krajcir's detailed confessions were outlined in the probable cause statement Swingle included with the warrant. A probable cause statement is an explanation of why a prosecutor believes the person he is charging is guilty of a crime. Without the confessions, it's unlikely Swingle could have charged Krajcir with all five murders, but getting the confessions hadn't come without a price. If the death penalty had been on the table, Krajcir would have taken his secrets to his grave. He knew he didn't have much left to live for, he once told Echols. But Krajcir didn't have a death wish, he had said, and he expressed his concern about confessing to any other crimes because he feared the death penalty, though it had been years since he'd actually enjoyed living.

———

The surviving relatives of each murder victim had forged a solid bond with one another over the years, and they all discussed the matter of Krajcir's fate over Thanksgiving the previous weekend. They all agreed that closure took priority over attempting to enforce the death penalty, and they surrendered to Krajcir's terms: he would live. The people he'd inflicted suffering on had lived with the horrors he'd caused for three decades, not knowing. Now he offered them a chance, perhaps their last chance, to put a face on the evil that had destroyed their lives. Most of the family members said it turned out to be the easiest decision they'd ever made.

———

By the time I faced Krajcir in that visitation room, he'd gained another sentence in addition to the one for the Sheppard homicide. This one was handed out after Krajcir copped to killing Virginia Lee Witte in 1978, a classy, attractive housewife from Marion, Illinois, about forty-five minutes from Cape Girardeau, Missouri. That conviction had earned Krajcir another forty years to be served consecutively, meaning the clock wouldn't start to run until he'd completed the first sentence. Everyone knew the man would never see the outside of a maximum security prison.

———

As a result, he now stood to serve multiple life sentences if convicted in Cape Girardeau, on top of the eighty years for the murders of the two Illinois women. His first murder charge was for killing Mary and Brenda Parsh, a mother and daughter, slain in their home in the summer of 1977. Sheila Cole, a college student about to graduate from Southeast Missouri State University, had been abducted from a Wal-Mart parking lot a few months later, and found dead in a rest-stop bathroom. Krajcir had also admitted to murdering Margie Call in 1982, and two months after Call's death, Mildred Wallace, who was found dead in her home in the same neighborhood. In between lay six more cold cases—five sexual assault crimes and one armed robbery, in which Krajcir had invaded the home of an elderly Cape Girardeau couple and threatened them out of their money.

The home invasion factor was Krajcir's trademark, though he'd also plucked several victims from grocery-store parking lots. The idea of preying on someone in their safe space, however, shattering any illusion they had of comfort, seemed to be his addiction. He almost seemed to thrive on depriving people of their right to feel secure in their own homes. He usually donned a blue bandanna to keep them from seeing his face, and so Morley Swingle had dubbed Krajcir the "bogeyman in the blue bandanna."

The Seabaughs, the couple whom he'd robbed in their own home, were tormented by their memories of Krajcir's brutality. The woman of the house later said her husband, Elza, had tried to stand his ground, but she'd forced him to back down. She made him give their hard-earned money to the man in the blue bandanna, caring more about her husband's safety than their cash. She'd feared for his life, but he'd feared for his manhood. The fact that he'd surrendered, and been overpowered in his own home, had plagued him until his death. He was never the same after that, his wife later said. Missouri has been what is known as a Castle Doctrine state for over a hundred years, by case law and now by statute. That is to say, its citizens have the right to use deadly force to protect their "castle" from a perceived threat. None of Krajcir's victims had been able to stop him from infiltrating their castle.

In addition to the Missouri cases, there were the deaths of Joyce Tharp, a pretty black woman abducted from her home in Paducah, Kentucky, in 1978, and Myrtle Rupp, slaughtered in her apartment in Pennsylvania in 1979. Krajcir had admitted to both those killings, but the crimes had yet to be tried.

During my visit, Detective Smith spoke quietly to Krajcir, making introductions. Jimmy Smith is a detective in the Cape Girardeau Police Department, and he dresses like one. No matter what the day's plans involve, Smith wears a suit to work. He doesn't dress any differently for daily work than he did for the myriad media interviews he'd garnered since the charges against Krajcir had been filed. The story had generated massive media attention— it's not every day that a small-town police department makes an arrest in five unsolved homicides. The horrific and baffling nature of those particular murders had haunted the town, and the police department, for thirty years. Smith had become a local celebrity, as, unfortunately, had Krajcir.

I received a polite nod from the convicted killer as I took my seat next to the sheriff's deputy.

"My name is Bridget DiCosmo, and I'm a reporter with the local newspaper," I said.

"Nice to meet you." Krajcir's reply was low and courteous, scarcely audible.

I recalled a conversation I'd had in Marion, Illinois, with Detective Tina Morrow, the officer who'd worked the homicide case of Virginia Lee Witte. Morrow is a tough cop, very self-possessed and professional, but I was curious. Given Timothy Krajcir's history as a sexual predator, had the thought crossed her mind that he might not respond well to being interviewed by a female detective?

"I wasn't worried about my safety, I was worried he may not be as cooperative with me as with Paul and Jimmy," she'd answered honestly, referring to detectives Paul Echols and Jimmy Smith. Morrow expressed the concern to Echols. He would know better than anyone. After months of work on the cases, Smith and Echols had more of a rapport with Krajcir than probably anyone else presently in the elderly inmate's life.

"[Echols] said it would be the easiest interview I ever did," Morrow had said.

Echols was right.

Whatever hatred Krajcir had toward women, hatred that came out in the heinous acts he perpetrated on his victims . . . you'd never know about it just from talking with the man. He gave succinct, one-word answers to my initial questions, capping each one off with a soft "ma'am."

"I understand you want to talk about Ida White, the woman who was stabbed in Mount Vernon in 1981," I said.

Krajcir nodded slowly. That attack was the only crime he was willing to discuss with any of the media. This desire to talk had been spawned by an interview Krajcir had done several weeks earlier with a detective from Mount Vernon, Illinois. Krajcir had confessed to several assaults in the moderately sized southern Illinois city, yet he couldn't manage to convince Mount Vernon authorities that he'd committed this crime. He'd convinced Echols and Smith, and me, as well as Stephen Swofford, the attorney for the man who'd been convicted of the stabbing, but he couldn't get anyone from the Mount Vernon Police Department to listen. The Illinois city lies directly across the river from St. Louis, and the police department there doesn't have too much interaction with Cape Girardeau law enforcement.

When the confessions had first started pouring from Krajcir's lips, Echols had informed Mount Vernon police chief Chris Mendenall that Krajcir had been talking about raping several women in the Mount Vernon area in the 1980s. He'd also described stabbing a woman in a basement apartment, in 1981. She hadn't died, at least not that Krajcir knew, but he recalled hurting her pretty badly. When Mendenall didn't respond to the heads-up, Echols finally put out a news release about Krajcir's confessions to several rapes in the Mount Vernon area during the early 1980s. Law enforcement put out feelers in nearly every jurisdiction within a hundred miles of the areas Krajcir had targeted during his salad days. They combed over records from every unsolved murder, home invasion, and rape that occurred from 1977 to 1983 in eastern Pennsylvania (the area where Krajcir grew up), southern Illinois, and western Kentucky. And, of course, they reopened files from cold cases in southeast Missouri, where Krajcir's blood trail began.

No stone was left unturned, every home invasion was checked out, every old, open rape case was combed over thoroughly for Krajcir's calling cards: the hands bound behind the back, the broken bathroom window, the blue bandanna.

Several active cases were solved that way, finally putting a name to the decades-old crimes, but there were still frustrations. Some of the rapes Krajcir told Echols and Smith about may have gone unreported when they happened, especially considering the attitudes toward sexual assault victims thirty years ago. Krajcir's memory may have slipped at times about dates and locations of incidents. Victims may have passed away. But while the two rapes and the sexual assault he'd talked about committing in Mount Vernon may have fallen into the unreported category, the stabbing did not. Within hours of receiving the news release, a television reporter found a news story on microfiche at the Mount Vernon library highlighting the arrest of a man for a 1981 stabbing identical to the one Krajcir described. That man's name was Grover Thompson, though, not Timothy Krajcir, and he had died in prison fifteen years after being convicted of the crime.

That's what Krajcir wanted to talk about. That's why I was here, inside the depressing visitation room instead of out in the late March sunshine. Because when Mendenall sent his detective to question Krajcir about the Mount Vernon rapes, the detective hadn't believed Krajcir's story about the stabbing. But the killer wanted credit, and he wanted the public to know about it.

The victim's name was Ida White. She'd been an older woman, and the attack had left her seriously injured. She could only testify at Thompson's trial after a lengthy hospital stay. She died years before Krajcir's name ever came up on police radar.

The attack on White bore an eerie resemblance to Krajcir's depiction of the stabbing he'd committed in the same city around the same time, down to the kind of night it had been and the layout of White's apartment. He hadn't known her name, of course—he never bothered to learn any of his victim's names—but the details he'd laid out for Echols and Smith were too specific for him to have known unless he'd been there.

The phrase *details only the perpetrator would have known* resurfaced constantly throughout the investigations. Though DNA tied Krajcir to several of the murders he'd committed, it was those confessions that ultimately convinced police and prosecutors that he was telling the truth. He spoke with authority about each crime, acting as if he held the key to mysteries that had taken decades to unravel, even if he couldn't possibly remember the address of the house or the name of the victim. It rankled Krajcir that the Mount Vernon detective hadn't believed him. He felt his credibility was at issue.

For a law enforcement agency, few nightmares are greater than having a conviction challenged, especially for a crime as serious and heinous as the attempted murder of an elderly woman. They already had a conviction in that case, and now it was being challenged through the media. Thompson's death only intensified the nightmare. People were rightfully upset at the thought that an innocent man may have died in prison.

Chief Mendenall had not been with the police department in 1981, but he firmly stood behind the arrest and subsequent conviction—a fact that needled Krajcir. When Mendenall found out that Grover Thompson had once been locked up at the Menard Psychiatric Center in Illinois, the same facility that had housed Krajcir for years, he thought the answer was obvious: Thompson clearly must have filled Krajcir in on the details of the assault, and there it was. A neat, tidy explanation—except that Krajcir vehemently denied it.

Leaning forward, I asked Krajcir why he was so concerned that Mount Vernon police didn't buy his confession.

"Because an innocent man died in prison," he said quickly. The response held the proper note of indignation.

A few questions more, and we got down to the root of the matter.

"He was just so arrogant," Krajcir said of the detective who'd interviewed him about the incident. Krajcir was frustrated. His entire body seemed to swell up out of the hard plastic chair, despite his restraints. The movement was far from threatening, but there was a self-righteousness about it that made me think of Anthony Hopkins's portrayal of Hannibal Lecter. It had taken a good deal of persuasion by detectives Echols and Smith to convince Krajcir to talk about any of the other crimes he'd committed, even after DNA pinned him to the one in Illinois. Only legal bargaining and the cooperation of victims' families to spare his life in exchange for closure loosened his tongue—but once he'd started, he'd been forthright. Now, it seemed his honesty was suddenly being called into question, and he wasn't pleased.

As the conversation continued, Krajcir took me through the whole night he'd surprised Ida White in her bathroom.

"I was exposing myself to a group of women outside the post office," he began, his tone no different from if he were discussing last night's Cardinals game. Besides the arrogance, that was the other thing that struck you right away about the man: he was capable of taking such a placid, matter-of-fact tone when talking about rape and murder. As polite, as courteous, as much of a gentleman as he was, his matter-of-fact way of speaking about his past exploits both unnerved and fascinated at the same time.

Ida White's Mount Vernon apartment was directly across the street from the post office, which was where police had discovered Grover Thompson after the attack, taking a nap in the lobby.

Krajcir explained that earlier that day, he'd been exposing himself across the street. He had a lengthy rap sheet citing similar incidents, in which he'd either been "Peeping Tomming," as he called it, or exposing his genitals. In fact, a psychiatrist at Menard, in diagnosing him as a repeat offender in those areas, concluded that he didn't believe Krajcir had the psychological makeup to even commit any of the more heinous crimes. He wasn't a hot reactor, doctors believed, and was therefore more likely to consider consequences. But they were dangerously mistaken—in fact, Krajcir had already committed at least five murders when that evaluation was done.

Voyeurism and exhibitionism had become so ingrained into Krajcir's routine that such acts seemed to precede many of his more villainous endeavors. The milder, more mischievous sex crimes seemed to be a type of foreplay for him, a way of getting him warmed up while he decided on a victim. After this, he'd usually move on to the rape or murder as the main event.

He'd noticed Ida White right after the flashing incident that day.

"I decided to do a sexual assault," he said.

Krajcir had committed a few home invasions during which he hadn't raped, hadn't preyed sexually on his victims, had limited himself to stealing, but it was extremely rare that he deviated from the threaten/rape/kill/leave pattern he'd established in 1977.

Ida lived in a basement apartment, and it was in speaking about it during the interview that Krajcir's memory, fuzzy at times, became sharpest. He mimicked his motions as he broke into the apartment through the bathroom window, demonstrating as best he could the act of lowering himself into the small space. He hid in the shower and waited for White to come home.

Looking back, he must have wondered how it was possible that he didn't get caught sooner. Dumb luck saved him time after time. Yet with each crime that went unsolved, Krajcir grew bolder.

The original investigators must have gone over a series of what-ifs hundreds of times after learning about Krajcir. What if they'd known that the link between most of the Cape Girardeau victims—after they'd considered everything from their initials to the streets they lived on—boiled down to something as simple as the corner grocery store? What if Krajcir had taken Sheila Cole, his third victim, back to her house to rape her instead of to his own trailer in Carbondale? What if Mary Parsh's husband hadn't been in the hospital?

As the interview wore on, Timothy Krajcir revealed glimpses of something that could be called charm, and of a sense of humor that made me see what had allowed Echols and Smith to develop a close rapport with him.

The Federal Bureau of Investigation debunks the profile stereotype of serial killers as degenerate drifters, and says they are just as likely to have a loving family at home whose members are clueless about their extracurricular activities. While Krajcir wasn't what you'd exactly call a pillar of the community, he was far from a derelict. He didn't have the charismatic charm associated with the likes of Ted Bundy, whom, Echols said, Krajcir idolized. Bundy had been a law student before his conviction for murder; in fact, he'd even done an impressive job of handling his own defense until the state introduced the bite-mark evidence that linked him to his victims. Only then had he requested an attorney.

Like Bundy, Krajcir had pursued a higher education, in his case studies in law enforcement, psychology, and forensics. He'd attended Southern Illinois University in Carbondale, where his major was criminal justice administration. For a minor, he'd selected psychology. Chillingly, current Cape Girardeau police chief Carl Kinnison and Lieutenant Paul Echols had attended the same college and had the same major during the same time as Krajcir. Neither man could recall ever seeing Krajcir in school, but agreed it was certainly possible their paths had crossed. Many of the core classes the three men would have been required to take would have been the same. Both Echols and Kinnison would go on to careers in police departments that would eventually bring Krajcir to justice. That all three men received the same education and may have even been in the same classes at one time was pure irony.

Krajcir became intimately familiar with the procedures of criminal investigations. The natural assumption was that someone who was taking classes in criminal justice and law enforcement by day, and stalking the streets raping and killing women by night, did so to learn how to evade detection. By immersing himself in the subject, Krajcir knew exactly what authorities were looking for at each of those crime scenes. He knew how to best dispose of the weapons, what to say to the victims he left alive to keep them quiet, how to keep his identity secret, how to avoid leaving fingerprints or physical evidence behind.

At least, that was the assumption. No one actually knew why Krajcir had decided to take the classes he had taken.

So I decided to ask.

"Why the criminal justice background?" I said.

He shrugged, as though he'd never really thought about it.

"I wanted to figure myself out," he replied, then paused for a split second before adding, "It didn't work."

Like all of his answers, it was nothing if not direct. Krajcir then spent a few minutes elaborating on his studies in developmental psychology, just to make sure he drove home the point that he had a very high IQ.

After the interview, as I was walking out of the visitation room, I turned and spoke.

"One more question. What's it like being back in Cape Girardeau, after so many years, and knowing everything you've done here?"

For the first time, Krajcir smiled. "Oh, it's wild," he said.

Chapter 1

Blue Bandanna

Timothy Wayne Krajcir was born in Mahoney City, Pennsylvania, in 1944, to unmarried parents. From the very beginning, his childhood was rocky, and things never really got much more stable for him. Krajcir never knew his father, who split when he was about a year old.

"My mom was only like sixteen I think and she had to find somebody to . . . you know, since she was out looking around again. And then she met my . . . my middle brother's [father]. And I guess she was with him for a long time. I don't know what happened to him at all," he later told Echols. But that relationship had ended as well, and then his mother met Bernie Krajcir when Timothy was about five or six years old. They had a son shortly after that, Krajcir's youngest brother. Bernie had done construction work for a living, a career choice that led to the family moving around a lot so he could find steady work. The situation left Krajcir with something of a rootless upbringing, and he later said he never really felt any sense of belonging anywhere growing up.

Although he never felt accepted by either his family or his classmates for various reasons, Krajcir was fortunate in one respect—his family wasn't poor, and he didn't want for much. The Krajcirs may not have been rich, but they were decently well-off. His stepfather worked hard, though that didn't leave him much time for the two sons he'd inherited when he wed Krajcir's mother.

Timothy's family finally settled, years later, in Ironton, Pennsylvania, a small town just north of Allentown. Allentown was one of the larger cities in the Keystone State, located in what was known as the Lehigh Valley region, nestled against the low-lying banks of the shallow Lehigh River. About a half hour north loomed the Pocono Mountains, a coal-mining region marked by several large ski resorts and scenic lakes. Ironton, on the rural fringes of the larger city, was poor. In the sixties and into the seventies, farmland still composed a significant portion of it.

Krajcir, a man who spent much of his adult life believing he was invincible, would later refer to his upbringing as his Achilles' heel. His mother was not abusive by any stretch of the imagination, but the perception of neglect was there—emotionally, if not physically. She devoted most of herself to her husband, forcing her children to accept the emotional leftovers. Though Timothy did have a father figure, his stepfather was completely dedicated to his work. When it came to finding friends, Timothy was left to fend for himself. He didn't do very well. As a result, he never developed any real skills when it came to forming relationships with people.

Perhaps it was because Timothy Krajcir always felt slightly neglected by his mother that he came to obsess over her. He claimed to prison psychiatrists that she would prance around the house in filmy negligees and lingerie, a vision that would serve as fodder for his earliest unhealthy fantasies. As early as adolescence, Krajcir thought about his mother in ways he knew were just not right. There existed a strong attraction, which an eleven-year-old boy knew he should not feel for his mother, but no one ever attempted to deal with it. By the age of fourteen, it manifested itself as sexually assertive behavior, though nothing as aggressive as what was to come much later.

Krajcir started with peeking at his mother's scantily clad form, but by adolescence, he'd graduated to ogling female neighbors and women he spotted in their yards or driveways. "Peeping Tomming," he called it. Voyeurism was a habit that a prison psychiatrist would later, wrongly, say separated Krajcir from more dangerous sexual predators. It was an innocent enough pursuit, they thought. Even though he graduated to flashing, exposing his privates, none of the doctors who evaluated him thought he was capable of actually harming anyone.

Years later, Krajcir would resort to acts of voyeurism and exhibitionism during times when he was struggling to keep himself from raping, or killing, again. Nearly every murder he committed was preceded by his flashing someone, usually a group of women, or spying on a potential victim.

Krajcir's sexual exploits escaped detection as he moved awkwardly into his teenage years. It wasn't that he didn't know how to relate to women; many described him as polite and charming, a real gentleman. He had girlfriends, and he had female friends, but they never crossed a certain emotional boundary he'd firmly established. A police report later described him as a white male with a very dark, Eastern European complexion. Slender build, about five-eight, one thirty. Thick black hair and thick eyebrows. Dark eyes. Soft-spoken and calm.

"That was me," Krajcir said.

He was only seventeen when he went into the navy, after a falling-out with his stepfather. "Yeah. Me and him didn't get along too good. Never did," Krajcir recalled to Echols. After an argument that came to blows, "Mom threw a suitcase at me and said get out. So . . . I split. Went to a place in Temple where I knew a couple. I had a good buddy over there and stayed there for a few days. Thought about things and then went home one night and told Mom to sign the papers for the navy. And that's it. I was gone," he said.

In the navy, for the first time, Krajcir found a place where his strength and athletic prowess helped him fit in. His career in the service was not unsuccessful, but it didn't last long. He was kicked out in 1961, when he raped for the first time—and got caught. The crime occurred in Lake County, Illinois.

The timing couldn't have been worse for Krajcir. He'd just gotten married to a girl named Barbara, and was about to become a father. They'd been together about six months. He'd been stationed at the Great Lakes, but he met her in Milwaukee, at an Eagles Club dance near Marquette University. She was still living with her parents, even though they'd gotten married. He had plans to join her when he got out of the navy, but the rape conviction interrupted those plans.

Barbara was carrying their child, but Krajcir was going to prison, Menard Psychiatric Center, one of the toughest penitentiaries in Illinois, for fifteen years for first-degree rape. At first, he and his young bride wrote to each other while he was in prison, but the letters eventually trailed off. "After about the second year that I was locked up, we decided the best thing to do would be split ways," Krajcir said.

Barbara had a baby girl, Charlotte,* in early summer in 1963. She never met her father.

If Krajcir had tendencies toward sexual violence when he'd gone to prison, they only worsened during the time he was around Illinois' most dangerous criminals. One man recalled that Krajcir kept to himself most of the time in prison, but he said Krajcir had scared him. He described him as an animal, void of emotion, a cold-blooded snake.

The portrayal would upset Krajcir, years later. It bothered him that people in the Heartland thought of him as a "monster who kills," as he was labeled in an editorial in the Cape Girardeau newspaper shortly after police announced the charges that had been filed against him.

"I'm not really like that, that's not who I am," he once told Echols.

---

*Denotes pseudonym.

"I love animals, I love children," he wanted to tell everyone.

When the Illinois Department of Corrections released Krajcir in 1978, they couldn't know they were freeing a man who'd started out dangerous and had become, through education, prison culture, and fifteen years of near solitude, the deadliest predator in the history of southeast Missouri.

Krajcir had lost his wife by the time he left prison. He'd never met his child, and never would. His wife moved to Milwaukee and began a new life with their little girl, one he would never be a part of. He communicated with her only through letters from that point on. The one relationship in his life that had a chance to be fulfilling, and it was over before it had ever really begun. Krajcir had no choice but to pick up and move on.

He moved to Carbondale, Illinois, a quiet urban college town, the home of Southern Illinois University, and took a job with the Jackson County Ambulance Service. While still in prison, Krajcir had begun taking college courses through SIU. He was able to walk with the class of 1974 at Shawnee College, and began working at a hospital shortly after that on work release. He'd worked in an empty obstetrics wing of that hospital, where, oddly enough, Echols had been born. The ambulance service was based out of that hospital, right across from the Carbondale police station. Krajcir used to play softball with some of the officers.

The job created a danger zone that may have tempted Krajcir too much. It took him too close to residential neighborhoods, and helped him familiarize himself with areas of town that single women gravitated toward. In short, it helped him pinpoint victims.

Krajcir raped again. It was a foolish, foolish decision and, he realized later, probably the stupidest one he'd ever made.

He'd only been out of prison for about eight or nine months, and he'd been doing okay. Not well, but decent. He had a girl, one he thought he could care about. She was married, but that didn't get in the way too much.

He was helping people, providing a real service for the community of Carbondale. Then, just when things were looking up, the girl had a change of heart. When she suddenly broke it off, Krajcir sank deeper and deeper. He was depressed, and that was never good. Not good for him, and especially not good for the women in the nearby community of Cape Girardeau, Missouri.

In the 1970s, Cape Girardeau was a bustling little town, sparkling against the shores of the Mighty Mississippi. Its location had long made it among the most desirable real estate near the Bootheel region of Missouri. The area was known for moderate temperatures, lush vegetation, and prime access to the Mississippi, as well as for its rich Native American heritage, having been home to the Ozark Bluff Dweller and Mississippian tribes.

Mark Twain recalled his brief encounter with the town of Cape Girardeau in *Life on the Mississippi,* in which he alludes to two of its educational institutions. "Cape Girardeau is situated on a hillside, and makes a handsome appearance," Twain wrote. He made reference to the St. Vincent's Seminary, a former Jesuit school at the foot of the river, which closed in 1979. The site now hosts the

Southeast Missouri State University River Campus and
Earl and Margie Holland's School of Visual and Performing Arts, snug up against the Bill Emerson Memorial Bridge into Illinois.

Twain mentioned another college, one "higher up on
an airy summit,—a bright new edifice, picturesquely and
peculiarly towered and pinnacled—a sort of gigantic cast-
ers, with the cruets all complete." That school of higher
learning was the Third District Normal School, a Victo-
rian building, which was devastated by fire and completely
destroyed in 1902.

Four years later, Southeast Missouri State College's
stately Academic Hall replaced the Normal School, its
distinctive domed appearance soon becoming a landmark
for the town of Cape Girardeau.

By the 1970s, the school boasted an enrollment of more
than seven thousand students. Most of them came from
other parts of Missouri and Illinois, but a few wandered
to Southeast from other parts of the country. The construction of Interstate 55, the highway that connects St.
Louis to the city of Cape Girardeau, low tuition rates,
and an aggressive approach to recruiting gradually ex-
panded the college until it became Southeast Missouri
State University in 1972. The school's curriculum now
includes programs in nursing, liberal arts, and business,
where previously its focus had been strictly education
courses. By 1975, the campus, nestled on the north side
of the city on a hilly patch of green, consisted of twenty-
two buildings. Many students still chose to live off campus, however.

The influx of students helped fuel a tourism industry

in Cape Girardeau that thrived on the natural charm and sense of history about the town.

At this time, Krajcir lived in a small trailer on Springer Street in Carbondale, Illinois, renting from the man who owned the yard. His landlord lived in a small house on the property with his wife and two adolescent daughters. Krajcir's job with the Jackson County Ambulance Service had brought him to Cape Girardeau's two major medical centers, Southeast Missouri Hospital and Saint Francis Medical Center a few times.

Whenever Krajcir sank to the depths of depression, he knew there was the danger of his going out and doing something bad. It was as though someone flipped a switch in his head, and the good, productive member of society, the model student, the model parolee, suddenly became the rapist, the one capable of killing again and again and again.

Although he hadn't committed a crime since walking out of prison, Krajcir chose the Mohr-Value store, a sprawling giant of a discount supermarket that had just been purchased by Wal-Mart as his hunting grounds that day in 1977. The vast parking lot gave him ample room to work. He could park his blue '69 Dodge Coronet on the outer fringes of the lot and observe every single woman who strode out of the glass doors. More women tended to shop alone at the big store than at Kroger's. At Kroger's they hung out in groups, making it much harder to single out one of them. It was difficult to say what exactly he was looking for in each potential victim.

The young black woman he saw that day looked to be in her late twenties and she was undeniably attractive, even in the poor light. She had a young daughter with her, about five years old. A light sprinkle pelted the windshield of Krajcir's car as he watched them. He glanced at the clock. It was around eight in the evening, and darkness had fallen over the parking lot. When he'd set out looking for a victim, he'd said to himself, "The first pretty girl I see, I'm going to take." This young mother certainly fit the bill, and the child was a mild problem who could be dealt with easily enough.

Krajcir fingered the knife. Before his target, Leslie Marcano,* could reach the safety of her vehicle, he was stepping out of his car. Time became a blur for Krajcir as he swung into action. He showed her the knife. Threatened her. Threatened the kid. "Do what I say," he told them. "I won't hurt you if you do what I say." He forced them into her car, but something about that didn't feel right. It had a much different feel than breaking into a woman's home and assaulting her there. Here, he felt much less in control. He forced his way into the car right after them. He'd rather do this in his own car. He felt like driving a ways, and he wanted to drive his own car. He had more control of the situation that way.

Threatening Leslie the whole time, with ugliness, with the knife, with violence, he forced her and her daughter into his car. He put the kid in the backseat of his little four-door coupe; the young girl lay down back there, unaware of the hell her mother, her protector, was going through at that moment, oblivious to the danger, the knife.

_____

*Denotes pseudonym.

30

Neither mother nor daughter put up too much of a fight, and he drove around for a while, no destination in mind, as the pain began to ebb away slowly from the center of his consciousness. The rain slicked down over the windshield as Krajcir maneuvered the Dodge along William Street, headed back toward Illinois.

"Take your clothes off," he ordered, as though it was a reasonable request.

Quietly, terror-stricken, the woman murmured a question, her voice hushed and halting with choked fear.

"Rather than . . . have intercourse with you . . . would you allow me to . . . do you . . . orally?"

Krajcir considered it for a brief second.

"Okay," he replied slowly.

She began to go down on him. It was good for a bit, and then he changed his mind. He told her to stop, and informed her it wasn't cutting it. He wanted to have sex with her. They got in the position, but at that moment the switch flipped again. They still hadn't left the car. Krajcir stopped. He allowed her to get dressed. He drove her and her daughter back to the store, and dropped them off by their car.

Before Krajcir left, he offered the woman some hush money. A bribe. All he had was a twenty, though. He felt bad. She deserved more. He apologized for not having more. "All of this?" Leslie asked, her tone somehow managing sarcasm in spite of her fear. To her, it felt like a threat. She was too frightened of her tormentor's return to report the incident to police.

She told Krajcir then that she was very religious, and that she would pray for him. It was an unusual thing for her to say, and it stuck with him. She got back into her car, and lay down across the front seat.

That assault, unreported and unwitnessed by anyone except the woman's daughter, introduced Cape Girardeau to Timothy Krajcir. But it wouldn't be the last time that the pretty young mother's path would cross Krajcir's, and the next time would be even more devastating for Leslie Marcano and her daughter.

Krajcir was a stranger to the Mississippi river community, but he would spend the next five years terrorizing its female population, without his name ever registering a blip of the radar of the local police departments or sheriff's office. Thirty years later, it would be a name that was synonymous with murder in Cape Girardeau.

Chapter 2

Death of a Beauty Queen

Timothy Krajcir had committed burglaries before. He was no stranger to home invasions; in fact, he'd come to appreciate the perverse sense of intimacy they somehow gave him. Touching someone's private, safe space, rifling through their personal belongings, gave him a sense of power.

But when he broke into the little shoe-box-style home on the corner of Springer Street in Carbondale, he found something new. Something that took the simple power he usually derived from breaking in and magnified it times ten.

Between a mattress and a box spring, Krajcir found a .38 Police Special undercover-model pistol. What use did the insurance salesman who lived here have for a gun? It had been no great shakes to get in through the basement window. The man was on vacation, he knew that. No one had come or gone for days. This wasn't even a bad neighborhood; Krajcir himself lived a block south.

Krajcir had frequently entertained the thought that what held him back from killing the women he raped was that he lacked a weapon. Oh, sure, he carried knives sometimes. He'd used a knife to commit the rape that had landed him in prison. But he'd never had a gun.

Adrenaline poured through his body as he fondled the revolver. Rape was all about the power, the control, and this felt no different. Taking that gun felt damn near close to raping a woman and it resonated with the potential of what he could do with it. No woman on earth would dare refuse him now, not while he carried that pistol.

Years later, he would regret ever having picked it up, but for now, he basked in the sense of renewed power it shot straight through him. He grabbed a box of ammunition on the way out.

———

Appearances could be deceiving. On the surface, Brenda Parsh was a stunning, dark-haired beauty, a real head turner, who had every reason to be vain about her looks. They had garnered the young woman a number of titles in beauty pageants during high school and college, including Watermelon Queen and runner-up in the Miss Missouri pageant. Pursuing drama classes at Southeast certainly didn't hurt. One of her classmates described an incident during a morning class one semester when Brenda swept into the room wearing a flowery dress and quietly took her seat.

The professor halted his lecture right then and there. "Why, Miz Brenda Pah'sh," he drawled in a southeast Missourian twang. "You look absolutely beautiful. Stand up and show the class," he instructed.

Blushing prettily, and more than a little flustered, Brenda stood and slowly twirled while the boys in the class twitched and fidgeted uncomfortably. She took her seat again.

As she did everything, Brenda handled the awkward situation with aplomb.

That was Brenda Parsh. She was as kind and open as she was beautiful. Though she'd dated Larry Johnston, the quarterback on the football team, throughout high school, she'd been nice to the nerds as well. Larry and Brenda had been the classic high school couple: the football star and the cheerleader. But shortly after graduating in 1967, they went their separate ways. Johnston joined the air force, a fairly common path for a boy from southeast Missouri, while Brenda pursued a career in fashion and a hobby in drama at Southeast Missouri State University, where she met fellow actor Rick McGougan and continued to garner titles in beauty pageants.

After college, Brenda and Rick lived together in St. Louis for about six months. Both clung to their dream of pursuing an acting career, but those dreams assumed different forms as Brenda began to model, slowly immersing herself in the growing fashion industry in the city. Rick took odd jobs to supplement his acting work.

After they'd been living together for a while, Rick came to think of Brenda as his fiancée, and would gladly have married her, but she wanted him to establish a solid career in acting, with a regular salary, before they wed. Rick and Brenda had been together for five or six years. She helped support him while he strove to get his acting career off the ground, something her parents didn't always like. Some family members described their relationship as "rocky." The couple argued frequently, but Rick never raised a hand to Brenda, and their arguments were never violent. Such dissension is perhaps typical of couples in their late twenties. Both had dreams and ambitions, and though each desperately tried to make room for the other, their lives were becoming more and more narrow.

Ultimately, they came to a mutual decision that Rick should move to the West Coast, to California, at least temporarily, and look for acting work, something steady. Brenda couldn't argue that there were a lot more acting opportunities out there than in the Midwest. She decided to accept a job as a clothes buyer in Milwaukee with a major retailer. It was a stepping-stone job, one that would hopefully lead to a successful modeling, or possibly acting, career, and she was good at it, and it meant she got to travel to New York and Chicago frequently. At this time Brenda had been out of college about four years.

Brenda's sister, Karen, lived in Chesterfield, Missouri, with her husband, Bruce Chesser. Three years Brenda's elder, Karen had the same dark hair, high cheekbones, and fair skin. Most people described Brenda as outgoing and Karen as more reserved and quiet.

Karen worked at Famous-Barr of St. Louis, the same department store where Brenda had worked until the summer of 1977. Though the girls lived away from home, they remained close to their mother. Bruce Chesser described his mother-in-law affectionately as the type to "smother you with love." Mary Parsh was extremely devoted to her two daughters, and it was a two-way street. They talked on the phone nearly every day, and visited as often as they could. Sometimes Bruce felt his mother-in-law harbored some resentment toward him because he wouldn't let Karen drive the hour and a half to Cape Girardeau to visit her every weekend.

When Brenda made plans to fly home to see her parents on August 9, 1977, from New York, where she'd been sent on assignment, she stopped in St. Louis to see Karen, even though it would be a brief visit. The girls' father, Floyd Parsh, was in the hospital after a recent heart attack, and Brenda intended to spend some time with him while she was home. She had also promised to drive her mother to Illinois for her fortieth high school reunion the following day.

Karen talked to her younger sister that Friday afternoon, when Brenda called from New York to let her know that she'd be arriving in St. Louis at around 5 P.M. Shortly after the girls hung up, Mary Parsh called Karen and asked if she knew when Brenda was getting in. Karen told her that she did, and that the sisters were planning on meeting up at the airport for a brief visit between Brenda's flights.

Karen then called Bruce and told him her plans for the afternoon, saying she should be home by 7:30 P.M.

Brenda was standing in the terminal when Karen arrived at the airport after work. Brenda wore a blue dress that Karen had made for her. The sisters shared a meal and caught up with each other, then went on to the Ambassador Club at the airport to talk.

Fog had slowly rolled in over the Mississippi that morning, and soon a steady drizzle began to fall, lasting until around noon. The sky cleared but remained dreary, the temperatures clinging to the low seventies by the time Brenda's plane arrived at Cape Girardeau.

Mary Parsh happily greeted her daughter at the airport, clad in a conservative white pantsuit trimmed in brown. She took Brenda's bags and they walked to Mary's Ford Galaxie. The two planned to drop off Brenda's luggage, change into more comfortable clothes, and visit Floyd Parsh in the hospital before bed time.

———

Timothy Krajcir never knew their names. He didn't know that Mary had daughters, or that Brenda would be there. He'd scouted the neighborhood one night, parked his car, and looked around. A dark blue bandanna, which would later become his signature killing gear, may have been snugly tied around the lower half of his face. Dusk had fallen on the Mississippi shore. He was Peeping Tomming, peeking in windows and garages. When he spotted Mary Parsh in the bedroom window toward the back of her house, he assumed she lived alone. He stayed for a while, and never saw a man enter or leave the premises.

The house was built like a shoe box, a brick rancher that sat well back from the drive at 612 Koch Street. The bedroom window through which Krajcir spied on Mary was at the back. He would wait a week, he decided. Then he would come back, armed with his new toy, and he would assault her.

Mary was older, but in good shape, if a little plump.

Tight ginger curls peppered with gray framed her face, and she dressed conservatively. She was a small woman, energetic, with high cheekbones, a smooth complexion, and a sprightly look that appealed to Krajcir.

The hour grew late as Krajcir waited inside the house for Mary to return, something that nagged him a bit. It was after ten. She didn't seem like the type to stay out so late on a weeknight. She had to work. He'd gotten into the ranch house by cracking the window in the back of the house. It was the kind of window that cranked outward. Krajcir had to put his coat against the window and use a rock to smash it. The window was a little far from the ground, and it took some athleticism to clamber into the house. Glass covered the floor. Krajcir tried to hide it by sweeping it closer to the window, just in case.

He waited about a half hour for the front door to open. When at last it did, he knew instantly that something was wrong. He heard voices. Sometimes Krajcir bolted when this happened, but that night he stood his ground. He heard the keys jangle on their chain, and then the two women were inside the house.

Krajcir waited in one of the bedrooms for the two women to move deeper into the house. He'd been caught off guard, but he was already inside. There was no going back now.

Maybe Brenda's unexpected presence was what turned the tide, transformed Krajcir from a rapist into a killer. Maybe the chance to strike out at an obvious mother figure was too tempting. Maybe it was simply the gun.

Mary led her younger daughter into the master bedroom so she could put her luggage down. Krajcir moved quietly through the house after them. They were still talking when he walked in. He appeared in the doorway of the master bedroom, effectively interrupting the reunion. Waving the gun, he herded Mary and Brenda into the other room, the one where he'd lain in wait.

"Do what I say, or someone will get hurt," Krajcir said. The words were a habit at this point. A threat, but really more of a plea for his victim to cooperate so nothing went wrong. So far, Krajcir hadn't had anything go terribly wrong. He'd been afraid that Leslie, the woman from the parking lot, would turn him in, but she hadn't.

He instructed the two women before him to kneel as he prepared to assault them. Mary had been his initial victim, the one he'd picked out. But once Brenda stood before him, he changed his mind. She was breathtakingly beautiful, even frightened half to death as she must have been.

The mother was scared. She began to panic, to holler, and her daughter spoke quietly to her, trying to calm her down. Finally, Krajcir struck Mary on the right side of her face, to make her be quiet, breaking a tooth and leaving an angry red bruise on her face.

He ordered the women to undress and sit on the bed. Both complied. He caressed Mary a bit while he laid her on the bed, but that was the extent of their sexual contact.

He assaulted Brenda, making her fellate him, then raping her. Mary cried quietly during her daughter's ordeal. While he had his penis inside Brenda's mouth, the phone rang. He let her get up to answer.

It was Floyd, calling from the hospital. It was late, after ten, and he assumed his wife and daughter would be back from the airport. They should have been at the hospital. The fact that he hadn't heard from them worried him considerably. He had to call because the hospital didn't allow incoming calls after ten.

When he heard Brenda's voice, Floyd knew something was wrong with his daughter. Her normally chatty, friendly voice sounded strained and tense. The inquisitiveness to which he'd grown accustomed while he was in the hospital had vanished. She'd usually fire questions at him, about his medications, his diet, what the doctors had to say, and their calls generally lasted for about a half hour.

This conversation was different. "She didn't sound like my Brenda," he recalled later.

"Hi, how are you?" Floyd asked his daughter, trying to tone down the anxiety in his voice.

"Fine, Daddy," Brenda replied. There was no lengthy apology or explanation as to why she and Mary hadn't stopped by the hospital on their way home from the airport, no question about his health.

"Let me talk to your mother," Floyd said.

"She's in the bathroom. Daddy, I'm really tired. I've flown from New York then down here and I'm tired. I'd like to go to bed," Brenda answered, her tone hushed. She paused several times while speaking, as if struggling to decide what to say next.

"Okay, bye." Floyd let his daughter off the phone.

"Bye, Daddy," Brenda said to her father, for the last time.

The conversation plagued Floyd Parsh for the rest of the night. He felt in his gut that something had gone terribly wrong, and he didn't get a lick of sleep.

Krajcir had lost interest in the conversation by the time Brenda hung up the phone.

He forced both woman onto their stomachs and searched the room for something handy to use to tie them. His eyes fell on the portable television sitting on a cedar chest of drawers. Pulling out his buck knife, he flipped open the blade and sawed through the television cord. He received a nasty shock in the process, but the cord, about eighteen inches of it, came away in his hands. He bound the two women's wrists tightly behind their backs.

In 1963, when Krajcir had been incarcerated at Menard Psychiatric Center for his first rape, he'd met a fellow convict named Todd Hopkins.[*] Hopkins was a dangerous man and a convicted killer. At the time he was serving a sentence for assault, but he would eventually slaughter his wife and another young girl in Illinois near Carbondale. Krajcir was only eighteen when he knew Hopkins, but they established a rapport. They used to spend hours talking about all sorts of things. Krajcir would never forget Todd's chilling advice: "Tim, if you ever do anything, don't leave no witnesses."

The words had stuck in Krajcir's mind for the past thirteen years. Now, faced with the possibility of two adult witnesses to his terrible deed, he realized he had both cause and means to follow the suggestion. Now he had a weapon.

Slowly, Krajcir raised the gun.

He knew he didn't really have a good reason to kill the

---

*Denotes pseudonym.

42

women. Mary and Brenda had never seen his face. The blue cotton bandanna would have effectively masked his features. He could be anyone, even someone they knew. He'd barely spoken to them, so even voice identification would be unlikely. And he knew he hadn't left any physical evidence behind, since he never ejaculated during the rape. Still, Hopkins's words kept running through his head, urging him to end any possible threat of being caught.

Looking at the gorgeous young girl and the attractive older woman, Hopkins's words floated through Krajcir's mind once more, the mantra driving his actions as he fired two shots, one at the back of each woman's head. Both women went still on the bed.

Krajcir left the room. He walked into another room and began pawing through their things, looking for guns and money. He found about sixty dollars in a wallet and pocketed the cash. Krajcir was getting ready to leave when he heard muffled sobbing coming from the bedroom.

Mary Parsh lay next to her daughter's lifeless body, chin pressed into the bedclothes, crying. Sobs racked her nude body, but she was still very much alive.

She may have been crying from fear, or from shock at the trauma of lying next to her dead baby girl. The sobs died down when her tormentor's burly frame appeared again in the doorway.

Krajcir was alarmed, and more than slightly surprised that the woman was alive, but he never let it faze him as he took aim with the little pistol. He fired another shot, and this one didn't miss. He shot Mary Parsh clean in the head. The bullet passed through her skull and buried itself in Brenda's body.

Krajcir boldly walked out of the Parsh residence through the front door.

When Karen didn't hear from her mother or sister the next day, she wasn't too concerned, knowing that Mary had had a hair appointment that morning and Brenda would've definitely gone straight to the hospital to see their father.

After that, Karen figured Brenda would drive Mary to her reunion in Alton, Illinois. It wasn't until Sunday evening that Karen began to get a niggling feeling that something was wrong. Her uncle, who lived in Alton, called to say that he was concerned because Mary should have contacted him to say she was in town. He'd gone to the Alton High School reunion and she hadn't shown up. He called the hotel he knew she'd be staying in and the front desk said she never checked in. They couldn't even locate a reservation.

Now Karen was upset. She frantically called her sister in Wisconsin and her parents in Cape Girardeau. She tried to call her father at the hospital, but couldn't get the switchboard to put her through. When she finally talked to him Monday, he was as worried as she was about their loved ones. "Sissy," as he called Brenda, should have stopped by to see him on Saturday, and she never showed. The idea that she would have left town without visiting her father just didn't fit. Something was very, very wrong. Floyd Parsh had been calling the house since Saturday, and no one had answered. When Karen hung up the phone, she talked to her husband, Bruce, about the situation. They both feared that Brenda and Mary had been involved in a car crash somewhere between Cape Girardeau and Alton. Bruce offered to call the state police in both Missouri and Illinois to find out whether anyone had reported an accident. No luck there.

Mr. Blattel, a nearby neighbor of Floyd and Mary, later swore that he'd heard gunshots Friday night, around ten or eleven. His wife insisted it must have been a car backfiring. Gunfire was something you didn't have to worry about in the quiet neighborhood. Most of the people who lived on Koch Street were elderly couples or families with small children.

But Mr. Blattel knew what he'd heard. He'd nearly called the police. Another neighbor had heard dogs barking frantically. The dogs lived on the other side of the Parsh home. Perhaps they just needed to be let out. More likely, they'd spied a dark-clad figure sauntering out the front door of the Parsh house, and knew he didn't belong there.

Mrs. Blattel was the one who eventually discovered the bodies. Karen had called her Monday and asked her to check on her mother and sister, because no one had heard from them, and she and Bruce were near panic with concern. Mrs. Blattel told Karen that she, too, was a little worried, because Mary's beast of a car had been parked in the carport all weekend, yet no one had heard a peep out of her. Mrs. Blattel agreed to take a peek at the house and see what was going on. What happened next was something she wouldn't be able to recall thirty years later without falling into a state of near hysterics.

Not only was Mary's car still in the carport, but two

August 14 newspapers, the local *Southeast Missourian* and the St. Louis paper, lay untouched on the doorstep. Tucked inside the front door was Friday's newspaper.

When Mrs. Blattel walked into the bedroom, her first thought was that two African-American women had been slain in the Parsh residence; the bodies were already so badly decayed that they had changed color. The sweltering August heat and stale un-air-conditioned room had done a number on them. Heat and moisture are the two things that can accelerate decomposition in a body. As she stared in horror at the crumpled forms, the reality of what she was looking at slowly began to register. She started to scream.

Three minutes later, another neighbor saw Mrs. Blattel fly out the door and into her own house, and knew something was terribly wrong. Mrs. Blattel made a beeline for the phone, and struggled to keep her voice calm and distant as she called Karen.

"You and your husband had better come to the Cape right away," Mrs. Blattel told Karen.

She refused to tell her what was wrong, but it was obvious from her voice. When Karen pressed the issue, Mrs. Blattel quietly confirmed everyone's worst fears. "They are both dead," she said.

Karen and Bruce took immediate leaves of absence from work before driving down to Cape Girardeau from Chesterfield. Then they called the house on Koch Street and spoke with a police officer who wouldn't release any information over the phone but advised them to come to the house as quickly as possible. Karen also placed a quick call to her father's physician, letting him know what had happened so that he could be present when Floyd learned that his wife and baby girl were dead.

Karen took charge of closing Brenda's two bank accounts and arranging to have her possessions shipped from Wisconsin. She promised police that if she found any type of journal or address book, she'd bring it to the police headquarters on Sprigg Street immediately.

Aside from a fortysomething white male who lived in the neighborhood and had always creeped out the Parsh girls, though they could never explain why, Karen couldn't give police information about anyone who'd want to harm her sister. Brenda Parsh simply had no enemies.

Karen's explanation of what had happened when she arrived home in Chesterfield after her meeting with Brenda at the airport duplicated that of her husband down to the letter, and came off almost as rehearsed. She said he messed around with his drawings until they retired for bed around 10:30 P.M.

Mary's friend and neighbor Vivian LaGrand told police she knew something was wrong when they noticed that the back window to the Parsh residence was wide open. Of course, closer inspection would have revealed that the window was actually broken, but even from afar she could tell something was off about the ranch house. Mary Parsh would have closed the window and turned on her air conditioner.

Vivian knew that Brenda was supposed to fly in to St. Louis from Milwaukee to visit her father in the hospital and drive her mother the 146 miles to her high school reunion. Mary worked for Vivian's husband as a keypunch operator at his trucking company. Mary was a creature of habit, and her routine consisted of heading home from work and going straight to the hospital to check on her husband, then sometimes returning to work until 9 P.M.

Vivian said she'd tried to call Mary Saturday morning, but no one had answered the phone. The LaGrands visited Floyd Parsh in the hospital that same morning. When Vivian pressed Floyd for information about Mary, the older man couldn't offer a logical explanation for her absence. In his condition, the last thing the LaGrands wanted to do was to upset him any more, so the topic was quickly dropped. That evening, they realized the lights were on in Mary's house, which further concerned them, and they called several times without an answer. Although concerned, the neighbors all seemed to assume that the house looked odd because no one was home, not because the occupants were inside dead.

Bruce Chesser called Rick McGougan immediately, thinking Brenda's longtime boyfriend deserved to know that she was dead, but he couldn't reach him. McGougan had been in St. Louis at the time of his girlfriend's death, visiting friends. It was fairly common knowledge that their relationship hadn't been at its highest point around this time. Brenda had told a friend the week before that things weren't going well, and were getting "unpleasant."

Still, though their relationship may have been on the rocks and their lives moving in different directions, Brenda's death devastated Rick. They hadn't seen each other since Brenda's move to Wisconsin a month earlier, but they wrote and called frequently. The last time McGougan had spoken with his girlfriend had been when she arrived at the St. Louis airport the night of her death. As had become custom, they'd argued, but only briefly. He hadn't received her message until her flight was about to depart, and he wanted to drive to Cape Girardeau to see her. Afraid his old clunker of a car would break down en route, Brenda had to tell him no, and he'd gotten upset. He went to his bartending job at Noah's Ark in St. Louis, and then went to visit relatives in nearby Florissant.

McGougan and the others were questioned first by responding officers, then a full-time detective handled the follow-up investigations. That was the way the department typically operated. With a crime of this magnitude, one of the higher-ranking detectives would be taking over.

The case was then assigned to Corporal John Brown of the Cape Girardeau Police Department. Back then, Brown led the detective division. One of the more bizarre leads he received while investigating the Parsh slaying involved a supposed confession by two lesbians. The information came from a female employee at Thorngate Limited, a plant that was a major employer in Cape Girardeau, who said she'd heard it from a friend of a friend. The way she understood it, two lesbians had committed the homicide because they were jealous of Brenda's boyfriend.

Meanwhile, those closest to Brenda and Mary were racking their brains trying to conjure up a legitimate motive for the brutal slayings. Bruce Chesser had taken to conducting his own investigation, calling several of Brenda's friends and asking them some questions about her work and private life. Some of those questions were a bit intrusive, those friends reported to police.

Trained investigators work a homicide in a circle, beginning with those closest to the victim and working outward, ruling out suspects as they go along. Karen's husband, Bruce, was heavily questioned, even submitting to a polygraph exam, but investigators couldn't find a single person who thought he would stray from his attractive and devoted wife.

Also inside that inner circle was Charles E. Steiver Jr., known to friends and family as Skip. Skip had been one of the more popular guys in Brenda's class at Cape Girardeau Central High School. He knew practically everyone in the graduating class, but he and Brenda had always been good friends. Platonic friends, but good friends. Two weeks before her death, they'd attended a tenth high school reunion as each other's "date." Afterward, they'd gone out with a group of old friends to the Purple Crackle, a raucous club over the bridge in McClure, Illinois. Steiver told police that Brenda had made a point of having lunch with him whenever she was in New York, where Steiver was a practicing attorney. The news of her death had to have hit him hard. He had been moving into a new apartment in New York City the weekend Brenda was killed. His girlfriend helped him unpack, and they had worked throughout the hot summer weekend.

Nearly every male who knew the Parsh women took a polygraph, back then considered the single most valuable investigative tool in eliminating suspects. They all registered as truthful. Polygraphs weren't known to be 100 percent accurate, but investigators tended to put more credence in them than they do today.

A murder that receives as much attention and becomes as high profile as that of the Parshes eventually seems to attract braggarts who claim to have inside information, even if it's just their imaginations working overtime, and this case was no exception. Rumors soon began trickling into the police department that several people had heard a local teenager, a sixteen-year-old boy, bragging at a party that he knew who had done the killing.

When the police called the boy out on his claim, he sheepishly admitted that he didn't have a clue who the guilty party was. He'd been at a party with some girls he knew from school. They were all terrified to be out at night because the killer was still at large, and he decided to have some fun with them. As a joke, he said he knew the murderer, and convinced one of his buddies to go along with the tasteless joke. He really just wanted to shake up the ladies a bit, get them good and scared. Once it became obvious he really didn't know anything about the murder, that particular line of investigation fizzled.

The investigation focused on Brenda, her friends, her boyfriends, her possible enemies. From the beginning, the slaying smacked of a revenge killing of some sort.

Mary Parsh's life had revolved around her family. She never drank, and she and Floyd were homebodies for the most part. Since her husband's illness, she'd been eating out much more frequently, then spending hours with him at the hospital before turning in for the night.

Some of Mary's coworkers at Inman Freight described her as very closemouthed about her personal life, her marriage in particular. When she'd had a bout with cancer seven years earlier, no one even knew about her illness until the day she entered the hospital for surgery. Mary worked at that company for fifteen years, and sometimes came across as slightly bossy, because she knew better than anyone how things were supposed to be run. Nevertheless, her coworkers couldn't recall a single real disagreement that anyone had with her.

Despite Mary's impeccable reputation, police had to ferret out every possibility, and sent an officer to every hotel in town and in neighboring cities, showing a photograph of her. Not surprisingly, she wasn't known at any of them, except the Sunny Hill Inn, where she frequently ate dinner in the restaurant, usually alone, but on occasion accompanied by one of her daughters.

Every young man living in the vicinity of Koch Street became suspect, and had police questioning their every move, hoping to shed light on the identity of the murderer.

Of all the suspects and potential suspects, one who came up on the radar flashing the strongest signal, even decades later, was Hank Treanor,[*] who lived nearby. By October of 1977, Hank, who was only eighteen years old, had been sent to Farmington for mental health treatment, on recommendation of his caseworker at Saint Francis Mental Health Center. He indicated to his caseworker at their meeting in October that he'd decided to move to Colorado and work on a ranch, because he'd done this kind of labor before and it appealed to him. Until he got on his feet, he was staying at a YMCA in town. Hank got

---

*Denotes pseudonym.

a job at Shivelbine's Music Store, a family-owned place on Broadway Street, and took classes in TV and radio repair at a vocational school. The caseworker considered his patient unstable, capable of violence, and it worried him that he was out on the streets.

One of Brenda's former high school classmates also hit the radar, because he'd tried unsuccessfully to date the pretty young woman, but that was ten years ago. Police grasped every straw they could find, but a thwarted date was a weak motive for such a brutal killing. The man hadn't seen Brenda in ten years, except for a brief glimpse at their reunion, when the crowd swirled too thick around the ex-cheerleader for him to even work his way over to say hello. A friend of his had actually dated her off and on throughout college, and the two men discussed the shocking news of Brenda's death. They both fondly remembered the striking brunette as having always been a lady. The news rocked the 1967 graduating class of Cape Girardeau Central High School.

Brenda had dated several men casually in between Johnston and McGougan, and one of them, a psychiatrist in Illinois who was on his honeymoon when Brenda was killed, said he considered Brenda to be an "attractive person, physically and personally." He described her as mature, direct, and very honest.

Ballistics results provided perhaps the only concrete lead in the case. The bullets had come from a .38-caliber revolver, likely a Charter Arms undercover model, though it could also have been a Rohm or R.G. The ammunition was found to be consistent with Remington-Peters. They showed eight land-groove markings, made in the barrel when fired, with a right twist. The specifications of the rifling were entered into a database that spat out the possible manufacturers. Only three firearms manufacturers could have produced the gun that fired bullets into the heads of Mary and Brenda Parsh, the Bureau of Alcohol, Tobacco and Firearms concluded.

Krajcir had left behind two distinct footprints amid the shattered glass when he'd entered through the window, but aside from that, investigators had little to go on in the way of physical evidence. He'd committed nearly the perfect crime, and August temperatures had taken care of any mishaps, the decaying bodies showing almost no physical material. Two decades before the regular use of CODIS, the national database where DNA samples of convicted felons are compiled for comparison with unknown material, investigators hadn't yet perfected a way of catching up with Krajcir. Unless, of course, he got sloppy—but that never happened.

The murder held the quaint neighborhood spellbound, paralyzed with fear. Normally welcoming folks now snapped door locks into place when a strange car cruised down the street and refused to allow police entry without seeing identification. Many women refused to answer the door during the day if they were home alone.

Nothing like this had ever before happened in Cape Girardeau. The last unsolved murder had been that of Bonnie Huffman, in 1954, way out in the country, not in town. Though Huffman's death remained one of Missouri's most celebrated mysteries, whoever had left the pretty young schoolteacher in a ditch, her neck broken, hadn't left such a demonic mark. Cape Girardeau had never experienced the type of evil that Krajcir brought, and it would get much darker.

The homicide investigation dragged on throughout the fall, and the leads, never overwhelming, slowly petered out. Brown officially became the lead investigator on the case in September, and hunted down several promising armed robbery or rape suspects known to have been in the area, but all of the searches turned out to be fruitless.

Hank Gerecke, Cape Girardeau's chief of police, grew more and more baffled by the case, and pursued the mystery relentlessly. One detective compared Gerecke's zeal to that of the character Joe Delaney in the Lawrence Sanders novel *The First Deadly Sin*. Gerecke chased leads from Massachusetts to California. He vowed never to consider the case closed until the murderer of Mary and Brenda Parsh was safely behind bars. A panel of psychiatrists from Saint Francis Medical Center examined the murder in an effort to create a profile of the killer. What they came up with didn't bear the slightest resemblance to Timothy Krajcir. The circumstances surrounding the women's death seemed so personal, so brutal, it was difficult to let go of the notion that it had been a revenge killing. Perhaps the idea of anyone being twisted enough to inflict such pain on random strangers was too horrible to entertain.

The further investigators probed into the lives of the Parsh women, however, the more they realized they had hit a dead end. No one had a motive to kill them. There was no torrid love affair, no scandalous secrets. Just two well-loved, normal women with friends, families, and men who adored them.

Three months later, Krajcir would give police a clue, when he killed again.

Chapter 3

Sheila

NOVEMBER 16, 1977

Sheila Cole arrived at the Algiers Lounge relatively early that night. She and a friend went to let loose and blow off some end-of-semester steam. She looked forward to a relaxing evening of shooting pool with some people she knew. Her friend made a round of introductions, and Sheila met a few new guys. Not that she was looking for anyone. She'd been dating the same boy for a while. At twenty-two and petite, 110 pounds, with looks most would call "cute," or even "impish," Sheila defined sweet. She had shiny, light brown hair cut just below her ears, creamy pale skin, and a delicate bone structure. The energetic coed was finishing up her zoology degree at Southeast Missouri State.

Sheila and her friends had a fun, laid-back night, going from one hangout to another, playing a few games of pool, and gathering more friends at each bar they visited. Things pretty much wrapped up by around midnight, and Sheila headed home to Sprigg Street with her friends.

Sheila lived off campus, right across the street from the Cape Girardeau Police Department. Sprigg Street was the main thoroughfare in Cape Girardeau. Most of the shops and local businesses, salons, restaurants, and offices had a Sprigg Street address. The neighborhood couldn't have been any safer, with several main public safety headquarters dotting the wide street. It was the last place people worried about crime.

Sheila woke up early and headed to an 8 A.M. class. She breezed through the day's classes, and met her boyfriend, Matt Sopko, at the campus. Matt didn't drive, so Sheila picked him up in her Chevy and they ate dinner at a McDonald's. Afterward, they stopped at Kroger's to pick up a few things, and Sheila took Matt home.

Their relationship seemed to be wearing thin, fraying at the edges a bit. They had been seeing each other for about seven months. Sheila had no doubts about Matt's affection, or about his loyalty. Lately, though, he always seemed to be getting on her case about something.

After taking Matt home, Sheila bounced through the Wal-Mart doors, her light brown hair swinging with her upbeat movements. She came out clutching a small shopping bag along with her purse. It held her freshly developed senior pictures, ready to be popped into the frames she'd purchased. She planned on giving them to friends and family as gifts.

Christmas was just around the corner. So was Sheila's last semester at Southeast Missouri State University. She headed toward her light blue Chevy Nova. Okay, so it actually belonged to her father. It felt like it was hers. The car was only a year old, and she'd been driving it most of that time.

The parking lot had been crowded when she'd gotten to the store, around 7:45 P.M., and then she'd had to wait in line. Now her car sat mostly alone on the outer fringes of the darkening parking lot. She'd parked alongside a large truck. If she hadn't done so, she might have seen the blue Dodge parked on the other side. She might have seen Krajcir sitting in the car, lurking on the outskirts of the lot. His car wasn't far from the same spot where he'd abducted the woman and her young daughter, terrorizing them for hours. Had Sheila known about that assault, maybe she would have been more cautious about where she'd parked that day.

Sheila slowed down slightly, giving the lot a quick once-over, then strode more briskly toward her car, fumbling for her keys. She managed to toss her package in the car and was about to slip into the driver's seat when a rustle behind her caught her attention. She might not have been able to see Krajcir slipping up behind the Nova from his hiding spot on the other side of the van, but she could have heard his heavy footsteps as he crept around the vehicle and took a firm grip of her elbow.

The scenario replayed itself just as before, and it would turn out to be an even graver mistake for Krajcir.

Krajcir waved the same gun he'd used to slay the Parsh women. Sheila Cole never screamed. There was no one around to hear her even if she had. Quiet, mute with terror, she followed Krajcir to his car. Wordlessly, he got behind the wheel, and put the Dodge in gear.

Krajcir turned right onto William Street, headed for the bridge into Illinois. Later, several people would swear they saw Sheila's car crossing over the river onto Illinois State Route 146 into McClure, less than a mile from where her body would eventually be found. They would be way off.

Krajcir forced Sheila to lie across the front seat, resting her head in his lap. He was beginning to like the feeling of having his victims lie that way. Perhaps the position lent a false sense of intimacy to the act, or maybe it was simply a matter of practicality, because he found he could better control their movements that way.

He kept the gun trained where Sheila could see it, its heavy presence not letting the girl forget the kind of danger that existed in that car. At some point during the drive, Krajcir may have relaxed enough with Sheila to let the gun slip down into the crack between the seat and the door on the left side of the driver's seat. She'd know it was there, know how quickly he could get to it if she made a move to escape. Not that she would've had a lot of options for escape at this point. Even if she managed to survive a fall from a moving vehicle, probably traveling at a decent clip of about sixty miles per hours along Route 3, houses were placed very sporadically along the deserted stretch of highway, stores and gas stations even farther apart. Only wide expanses of soybeans and wheat fields marked the rapidly diminishing miles toward Carbondale, where Krajcir was headed.

Krajcir would later tell police he didn't like to kill in

his own backyard. The same time he murdered Sheila, he had begun molesting an eleven-year-old girl, an ongoing series of abuse episodes that would span the next two years. Nevertheless, he chose to bring Sheila Cole into his tiny trailer in Carbondale. Thinking back on the assault, he later said he knew it was a dumb mistake, the kind that could have easily gotten him caught. Any of his friends could have walked into his trailer, they did that frequently, and how would he have explained the unwilling, scared-stiff girl, the gun that lay nearby? He wasn't thinking clearly, not when he got in one of these moods, and everything he knew about law enforcement and the principles of detection from his classes seemed to fly right out the window.

The sexual assault wasn't planned. At this point in his life, it seemed he either planned them meticulously, as with the Parsh women, or not at all. Sometimes they happened on the spur of the moment, and he'd have little warning about when or where he'd feel compelled to hurt someone. When it happened, he felt like he had very little real control over the outcome, as though his muscles moved independently of his mind.

"Just be quiet, and I won't hurt you," he told Sheila as he guided her out of the car and pushed her toward the trailer. Numbly, she obeyed, walking into the trailer. He asked her to disrobe. She hesitated, but again, he pointed the gun, and she took off her clothes. Krajcir spent a few minutes molesting her, groping her, before abusing her further, forcing her to give him oral sex.

Krajcir didn't think he left behind any evidence of the torture he'd inflicted on Sheila. He thought he'd been careful. But there was a trace of sperm on her jacket that would later be available for a possible comparison. He'd asked her to undress, and she had. He hadn't realized that doing so would mean her clothes lay on the floor, and could easily have gotten stained with his semen at some point during the assault.

They were there for less than forty-five minutes.

"I'll take you home," Krajcir promised when he finally allowed the girl to get dressed.

They talked very little on the drive. Krajcir didn't really know what to say. The car ride was tense and awkward. He asked enough questions to find out that Sheila lived with two roommates, and was in college.

They were almost back to Cape Girardeau when Krajcir's thought process changed. Up to this moment, he'd thought he was going to "do a sexual assault," but now they reached the point where something was going to go wrong. Sheila hadn't done anything to irritate him, hadn't done anything wrong that night. She had been, as it were, a model victim, and had gone along with all of his wishes, all of his orders, perfectly.

Still, Hopkins's words lingered in Krajcir's head, and he couldn't seem to get them out, no matter what he did.

"No witness, Tim," Hopkins had said.

When they neared the rest stop on Route 3, Krajcir decided to pull over. Again, it wasn't something he'd planned on doing, but once he stepped out of that Dodge, his intentions became clear, to himself, if not to Sheila. He was going to kill her.

The rest stop in McClure consisted of nothing but a small, wooden building, low to the ground, and a couple of maps denoting certain points of interest, such as nearby Horseshoe Lake, a wildlife refuge.

Krajcir dragged Sheila into the restroom with him, and she went willingly. That was where he shot her, point-blank, and without warning. Sheila's blood splattered the walls of the rest stop. Krajcir briefly rifled through her purse, but took nothing before tossing it into a trash receptacle, one of the most callous ways he ever discarded any of his victims' belongings.

On his way back to Carbondale, Krajcir later told police, he took a detour to dispose of the gun. He described tossing the revolver over the bridge and letting the Mississippi current carry it away.

Sheer luck led police to the body quickly. A tourist passing through Alexander County happened to need the facilities at the rest stop on Route 3. It was around 7 A.M., and hardly any traffic rolled by on the quiet state road as she parked her vehicle by the rustic wooden building. Sheila lay curled against the sink, her hands still shoved in the pockets of her yellow jacket. A look of horror was etched on her face, nearly disguised by the rivulets of blood that cascaded from wounds on her face and somewhere behind her head. Her light brown hair rested in a pool of barely congealed blood. She was fully dressed, in brown corduroy pants, a red, blue, and yellow checkered shirt, and brown shoes.

No one ever discovered the identity of the anonymous caller who reported the homicide. She only identified herself as a tourist. The same grisly scene greeted an Alexander County deputy when he arrived at the rest stop at 7:30 A.M., acting on the tip from the unknown caller.

Two deputies from the Alexander County Sheriff's Department later found Sheila's purse in the trash receptacle, which was how they identified the victim. Sheila Ellen Cole's life had been reduced to numbers on the Missouri driver's license and other cards in her wallet: birthdate, address, license number, Social Security number. Two partial shoe prints were discovered near the trash can.

The items discovered in her purse were typical of the type of girl Sheila had been—smart, organized, practical. Police retrieved a well-balanced checkbook, complete with daily expense record, a notebook and a couple of ballpoint pens, a small flashlight, a box of matches, just in case, and an envelope filled with coupons. The small amount of cash, just over ten dollars, traveler's checks, and a credit card discounted robbery as a motive for the brutal slaying.

Because the abduction occurred in Missouri and the murder in Illinois, the homicide became a matter of federal interest. Investigators from the Federal Bureau of Investigation were called in to work on the case, since kidnapping is both a state and a federal charge when it involves the crossing of state lines.

The autopsy revealed little about what had happened to Sheila Cole. Her clothing was removed and tested for the presence of semen or blood, aside from her own. Blood splatters speckled the front of her yellow jacket. The brown cords she had on did not appear to have bloodstains on them, but further testing would detect the presence of blood.

The bullet wounds were measured and found to be the same size on entry. The exit wound on the girl's face, a gaping wound through her forehead, was twice the size of the one in the back of her skull. The bullet had fractured the frontal part of her skull. Powder burns marred her creamy, porcelain skin.

A patrol officer from the Cape Girardeau Police Department took Sheila's Nova from the Wal-Mart parking lot to the Southeast Missouri Regional Crime Lab for processing. The car helped investigators trace Sheila's last steps on earth before she had gotten into Krajcir's car. They recovered her Wal-Mart purchases, still in the paper bag, and her cash-register receipt. Police interviewed the cashier whose name was on the ticket. She knew she must have rung up the purchases, but she didn't remember Sheila. Soil and rock samples were taken from the car. The floor mats were removed. The ashtray's contents were emptied. The cigarette butts were sprayed for prints—fruitlessly. The butts were of the same brands preferred by the victim and her boyfriend.

Several hair samples were taken from the people closest to Sheila and compared to those found in the Nova. Police retrieved samples from Sheila, Matt, and Connie Walker, Sheila's roommate. The hairs found in the car were consistent with Sheila and Matt's, which proved nothing, except to corroborate Matt's story that Sheila had picked him up earlier that night.

Investigators removed the entire wall of the women's restroom at the rest stop so that the wooden panel could be examined for bullets and trace evidence. They recovered an empty Olympia beer can and a hubcap from a Chevrolet, the same kind of car Sheila drove. Both were dead ends.

The only significant finding was the bullets. They were sent along to the FBI crime lab in Washington, D.C., along with the bullets from the Parsh slaying. Both were .38-caliber Remington-Peters bullets. Three bullets had been recovered from the Cole homicide. The bullets shared eight lands and grooves with a right twist. One of the bullets was mutilated to the point of uselessness in terms of forensic examination. The rifling impressions left when it was projected from a gun into Sheila Cole's body were scarred and disfigured beyond identification for comparison purposes. The bullets were of the identical caliber and brand—fifteen-grain, round-nosed bullets. And all had been fired from the same make and model of pistol, a Charter Arms .38-caliber undercover-model firearm.

Lab results confirmed that the bullets in both the Parsh and Cole homicides had indeed come from the same pistol. The science used to make this identification wasn't exact, but it was the second strongest piece of physical evidence investigators had to go on. For the first time in either case, they had a tangible lead. Sheila Cole's death was not an isolated incident, and neither, it appeared, was the Parsh killing. Yet they had to face facts. They had a killer who had struck more than once, yet they had no idea of his identity, and there was no way of stopping him from killing again.

Still, the bullets were not the biggest clue to the identity of Sheila's killer. The biggest clue was concealed in her clothing, and it would not be discovered for thirty years. Semen stained the seat of Sheila's brown cords, and the white underpants she'd worn were stained with both blood and sperm.

Sheila's parents, Mr. and Mrs. Harold Cole, were absolutely devastated and mystified by their daughter's murder. Sheila had not been the beauty queen that Brenda Parsh was, but she was attractive, smart, friendly, and there was something about her personality and smile that seemed to bewitch the boys. She was sweet-natured and generous, but also had a slightly edgy, independent side that boys found both alluring and frustrating. Sheila had a few ex-boyfriends, but ten times as many friends. Jerry Seegers, one of her exes, even contacted the FBI himself and offered to assist in bringing Sheila's killer to justice.

Seegers had dated Sheila for about two years while they both attended Meramac Community College in Kirkwood, Missouri. When Sheila left for Southeast, Seegers transferred to Southern Illinois University at Carbondale, Krajcir's school. Then, in January of 1977, Sheila broke off their relationship abruptly. Seegers received a letter from her saying she was "promised" to someone else.

The last time the two saw each other was about a month before Sheila sent the letter. Sheila had stayed with Seegers in the hotel room he'd rented in Cape Girardeau. They'd had dinner, gotten caught up, and gone for a hike at Trail of Tears National Park before returning to the hotel and watching television for the rest of the night. They'd never been sexually active, Seegers told police.

During a conversation in the summer of 1977, Sheila admitted to Seegers that she felt a little disillusioned about her current relationship with Matt Sopko. She complained that he gave her a hard time about her unladylike language and her smoking, though he himself smoked.

Police later confiscated a note they found on Matt Sopko's desk. In the note, Sopko told Sheila he loved her, but that he didn't think she needed him. The note, a perfectly innocent expression of Sopko's frustration in the relationship, seemed ominous in the wake of Sheila's death, especially considering the circumstances under which she died.

Seegers described Sheila as timid, and thought she considered herself totally defenseless. He doubted she would have been capable of standing up to an attacker. She'd been very fearful of water.

When Seegers learned of his ex-girlfriend's death, he immediately penned a letter to the then governor of Illinois, urging him to launch a full-scale investigation. Like all of Sheila's loved ones, Jerry Seegers craved answers.

Matt Sopko had had to identify Sheila's body. He was taken to the Crain-Barkett Funeral Home in Cairo, Illinois, about a forty-five-minute ride from Cape Girardeau, and forced to confront his girlfriend's corpse. Matt lived in Towers Complex, the main dormitory building at Southeast, but he slept over at Sheila's place three or four times a week. He was the last person to see Sheila alive. They'd been a close twosome, he told police.

Connie Walker, Sheila's roommate, hadn't seen her friend at all that day. She'd left the apartment at about noon, and Sheila was gone at that time. She'd last seen her the night before, November 15, and done some mild partying at some of the downtown bars, what passed for a nightlife in Cape Girardeau. The girls lived in a nice, brick apartment building on Sprigg Street. The neighborhood was more than safe—it was directly across the street from police headquarters.

Joan Barnard also lived in the building. She was one of the first people contacted by the police with the tragic news.

The last time she'd seen Sheila was around three-thirty in the afternoon the day before, at home, she said. Her bed had not been slept in.

The boys who lived downstairs hadn't seen Sheila since 9 A.M., when she'd bounced out of the house headed to the campus five blocks away for her animal-husbandry class.

One of the roommates did recall seeing the Nova parked outside around dinnertime, though. Another thought he remembered seeing Sheila standing by her car with a man, who he believed was her boyfriend, but he wasn't certain. It was while he was watching *Charlie's Angels,* he remembered. Another roommate recalled Sheila had left saying she was going to Wal-Mart to pick up some photos. Kroger's grocery store, which later became one of Krajcir's hunting grounds, was one of the last places Sheila had gone the day she vanished, Matt told police. They'd driven there together after having dinner. Then Sheila had taken Matt back to campus, where he ate a second time at the cafeteria with his roommate.

The Coles couldn't think of any enemies who would be considered serious suspects.

A coed named Dixie Gail Kenna gave police some more legitimate, or at least practical, leads. Kenna had lived with Sheila during the 1975–1976 school year, in a dorm, where Kenna still resided. Kenna told police about an ex-boyfriend of Sheila's named Little Z, a member of Sigma Tau Gamma fraternity. Little Z was very different from Matt Sopko, and contradicted a lot of what investigators had learned about Sheila's personality. She seemed to go for good boys, studious ones, if her past two boyfriends were any example. Little Z did not match that description. Some of Sheila's friends told police that he liked to party a lot.

Kenna told the police that she and Sheila "ran around" together even after Sheila got her own apartment, and that Sheila was also close with two other girls, Sue Large and Karen M. Higgins. The police interviewed over a hundred people in the hopes of finding someone, anyone, who could shed light on what happened to Sheila. Her death had become a horrible, cruel mystery that haunted her parents, brother, and sister for thirty years. For years, Harold Cole would periodically drive the streets of Cape Girardeau, though he lived several hours away, searching for something, anything, that might give insight into his daughter's death.

There were a number of leads that ultimately went nowhere. Tim Roth, a late-night deejay at KGMO, Cape's main radio station, got a phone call one night from a female caller. Roth was accustomed to getting all the weirdos and crackpots on his shift. This one sounded like she hadn't slept in days. She identified herself as "Barb."

"Have you learned about the murder?" asked Barb.

When Roth hesitated, she added, "Everybody needs a challenge."

The call needled Roth to the point where he called the

FBI. Barb had also told him during their short conversation that she lived in a trailer. He could hear a child making noise in the background during the phone call.

Alvin Charles was one of those witnesses who thought he could help. He lived on a gravel road near the Route 3 rest stop in McClure. Charles spoke with police the same day Sheila's body was discovered. He told them he recalled hearing a car with a noisy muffler rip down the road at a high rate of speed just before nine-thirty the previous evening.

Another person remembered hearing a gunshot about a half hour after Charles said he heard the car.

Gary Sperling, who worked at the Phillips 66 gas station and convenience store, remembered seeing a four-door Chrysler sedan parked at the rest stop. Sperling said he saw someone in uniform walking around in the parking lot near the car. This was around ten-thirty or eleven at night, hours after Cole left her house to go shopping.

A couple driving through McClure recalled seeing a blue midsize car, but there wasn't a soul around, they told investigators.

David Wright, a deputy in Alexander County, was on patrol during the wee small hours of the morning of November 17. He eased his patrol vehicle at a good clip down Route 3 in McClure, pulling into the rest stop to use the bathroom. The parking lot was deserted, as was the restroom he used. It was unclear whether or not Sheila Cole's body actually lay in the other restroom while he was there.

Another tip involved the Purple Crackle, a club across the river in Illinois with a somewhat unsavory reputation.

A man named "Johnny," who was in his fifties, allegedly tried to pressure a woman into going out with him, the police learned through a tip. When the woman he was talking to refused his advances, he told her she should change her mind because she didn't want to "wind up like the girl in the rest area."

One of the more chilling calls investigators received with regards to the Cole homicide involved a woman's possible brush with Sheila's killer, or so she thought. Over a year after Sheila's death, Jane Keller stopped at the now infamous rest stop in McClure around 8:30 A.M. When she got out of her car and walked into the women's restroom, she found a note. "If you want to fuck, I have eight inches and I am with you now," the note read. Jane continued to read the instructions to leave her name and number. The pervert would call, he said. The note was signed, simply, "David." She heard the door slam loudly in the adjacent men's room. When she stepped out of the ladies' room, the men's-room door also opened, and a man stood in the doorway. She described him as "scary." Jane began striding briskly toward her car. Footsteps picked up the pace behind her. She walked faster. The steps picked up as well. Jane nearly broke into a run before a maintenance truck from the Illinois Department of Transportation pulled into the rest stop.

The man from the restroom hopped in his car and left. Jane was shaking. She'd gotten a good look at him when he got into his vehicle. He was short, only about five three, and midthirties, with medium long dark hair, like a hippie, but neatly dressed in a light blue suit and tie and an off-white shirt. The car he slid into had a metallic frame, a dark blue color with lots of chrome, and Missouri plates. Normally Jane wouldn't have bothered to report the incident to authorities. Then she remembered Sheila's death.

Jane went to the Union County Sheriff's Department and described the incident. They took it seriously enough to send a deputy to check out the restroom. Deputies from the county sheriff's department had made scores of trips to this public bathroom over the previous two years. By the time a state trooper showed up, however, acting on Jane's tip, the note had vanished.

A deputy from the sheriff's department in Alexander County distinctly recalled seeing a blue Volkswagen in the parking lot of the rest area the night Sheila disappeared. A man and a woman left the car and walked around to the front of it as he drove by, he told investigators.

MAY 12, 1978

The murder of Virginia Lee Witte was one of Krajcir's boldest. Perhaps the success with the first three had gone to his head. The classy, raven-haired housewife was unloading groceries from the trunk of her car in the late-afternoon sunshine when Krajcir spotted her.

The Wittes had recently moved to Marion, Illinois, for work, and Virginia and her husband lived in a very nice, middle-class neighborhood. Virginia was seen by her neighbor, returning home from a trip to the grocery store in the early evening. There was no reason for Virginia to be glancing over her shoulder. She had no idea she was being watched by a killer. Her husband had returned to his office to do some work.

Krajcir chose not to shoot Virginia after he assaulted her in her own home. He was becoming adept at threatening his victims even without the gun. Again, perhaps the lack of repercussions for his heinous crimes was making him more confident.

Instead, he used one of Virginia's own knives, plucked out of her kitchen, to stab her. Then he strangled her to death and left her ravaged body for her husband to find when he returned home.

Krajcir left a lot of evidence behind in the Witte household. Police were able to retrieve more than a hundred pieces of forensic evidence from the crime scene—though it would nevertheless be decades before the crime was solved.

MAY 25, 1978

An assistant warden at Menard Correctional Center turned three .38-caliber Charter Arms pistols over to the Federal Bureau of Investigation. Investigators thought they might have found the weapon used in the Cole and the Parsh killings. Alas, the guns turned out to be another bogus lead, another false hope that didn't pan out. The following day, they were all returned to Menard, the prison where Timothy Krajcir had served fifteen years for rape. Officers and agents investigating the Cole homicide would look at over a dozen more Charter Arms pistols, all fruitlessly.

One of the guns initially seemed like a promising lead. It had belonged to an inmate who was in jail for armed robbery. He'd had the gun in his possession at the time police picked him up. Detective John Brown interviewed the man after learning that he'd registered a positive response to a polygraph examination when the subject of the Cape Girardeau homicides came up. He was also a suspect in the rape of a college student at Western Illinois University in Macomb, and during the lie detector analysis had ticked an affirmative response to a reference to a rape at Murray State University in Kentucky. During the interview, Brown worked out of him the information that he'd been suspended from a local university in 1978 for harassing and scaring two female students, and he was also being investigated as the suspected tormentor of two female students at Southern Illinois University. But there was nothing strong enough to link him to Sheila's death, no indication that their paths had even crossed. Sheila's roommate told police she had never heard of the man, and certainly didn't think that Sheila had known him. In the end, there wasn't enough evidence to implicate him in the campus rape. He voluntarily checked himself into a mental health center.

Investigating Sheila's homicide brought Brown and the other detectives into contact with some of the most unsavory and unscrupulous characters in southern Illinois and southeast Missouri. One man was suspected of kidnapping a woman in central Illinois. In 1979, Detective Ed Barker got a lead. A twenty-five-year-old man from Sikeston, Missouri, had just been charged with public indecency for exposing his genitals to a woman in the

parking lot of a grocery store in Marion, Illinois. The
information sounded like it had possibilities, more so
when Barker learned the man had attended SEMO, as
Southeast Missouri State was known, the same year the
Cole girl was killed.

On June 10, 1980, an inmate in Houston, Texas, began
bragging that he was wanted by authorities for a murder
he'd done in a place called Cape Girardeau, Missouri.
Texas law enforcement contacted the Cape Girardeau Police Department. Special Agent Lummus, a federal agent
investigating the case, contacted the FBI in Houston and
requested that the feds interview the prisoner. Nothing
came of it.

The next solid lead didn't come until about seven years
later, when Detective Brown and a local sheriff went
down to Florida to interview Ottis E. Toole, a man facing
about thirty various felony charges in the state. Toole
willingly discussed the Cole homicide with the two men.
He described traversing the country with his partner in
crime, Henry Lee Lucas, and claimed he'd killed one
hundred people by himself, and about sixty with Lucas.

He killed for sex and for money, often dressing like a
female to make it easier to approach victims, he told the
two officers. Toole said that he had been killing since the
age of fourteen. He and Lucas went through about ten
different vehicles during their travels to avoid detection,
and his partner often kept him confused about what state
or city they happened to be in, he said.

The police officers, needless to say, were skeptical

about the alleged killing spree. However, Toole and Lucas's MO was to kidnap women from parking lots as they were walking to their cars, Toole said, and his depiction of the murders he claimed to have committed was eerily similar to Krajcir's slayings. He even recalled kidnapping women from Wal-Marts on several occasions. But after looking at the photographs from the crime scene, in which Sheila lay in a pool of blood, he couldn't remember committing the crime, though he admitted that the pattern seemed to fit something he and Lucas would do. Brown and the sheriff went on to interview Henry Lee Lucas, once widely known as America's most prolific serial killer. Lucas claimed—then later recanted—to have committed around 600 murders; a group of Texas law enforcement officers organized a task force to examine the allegation, and deemed about 350 believable, but a former Texas attorney general criticized the task force and denounced Lucas as a liar, calling the whole string of confessions a big hoax. In 1998, then governor George W. Bush reduced Lucas's death sentence to life without the possibility of parole—the only time Bush ever intervened in a Texas death penalty case.

Sheila Cole's homicide began to frustrate officers even more than the Parsh slaying had. The investigation took on a different tone. In the Parsh homicide, the primary suspects had all been those closest to the victims, but Sheila Cole's death seemed to indicate a random, senseless act of violence. It was years before police even knew she'd been sexually assaulted; the autopsy didn't confirm any such abuse, and news reports actually indicated that she had not been raped or attacked in such a manner.

The longer Sheila's death went unexplained, the more frustrated her family grew with the investigation, and with the media. Every lead seemed to produce another dead end, though Detective Brown checked out every one that crossed his desk. The trail grew colder and colder with each passing year. Few women in Cape Girardeau ever forgot Sheila's brutal slaying, though. Every time they would drive past the rest area, closed a short time after the murder, the slain coed would cross their mind. By the time Krajcir struck again in Cape Girardeau five years later, police were no closer to resolving Sheila's murder.

———————

Timothy Krajcir's next victim, in March 1979, was Joyce Tharp, a beautiful black woman who lived in the neighborhood of Paducah, Kentucky, known as Forest Hills. She was the second woman whom Krajcir abducted and actually took somewhere to kill. Krajcir had cruised around Paducah that night, looking for the perfect victim. He had only one goal on his mind.

Attractive and alone were really his two biggest qualifications, but when he spied Joyce, he knew he'd found his prey for that evening. Joyce didn't actually live alone at the time. Her brother lived with her, but he'd spent the night at a girlfriend's house. Krajcir lingered a few minutes outside, watching Joyce sleep. A sleep mask shielded her eyes from the light filtering into her bedroom. She was one of a number of Krajcir's victims who happened to be black; nearly half of his victims were. A large percentage of the rest were older white women, who may have reminded Krajcir of his mother.

Krajcir slipped into Joyce's apartment through the window. He surprised her, brandishing a knife as he rousted her from her sleep. If she cooperated, she wouldn't be harmed, he promised, threatening her with the blade the whole time he herded her outside and into the car. They drove to his trailer in Carbondale, in an area known as the Crossings. There, he forced her to pleasure him, as he'd done with so many other victims, and then strangled her to death. He dumped her body into the trunk of the car, and calmly drove her back across state lines.

When he returned to Paducah, Krajcir dumped Joyce's nude body in a trash can behind a church. It was the wee hours of the morning, and pitch-black. Although the alley was deserted, carrying a dead woman from the trunk of a car into a relatively large and populated city was still a bold move.

Joyce's body was discovered in the trash can thirty hours later, buckets of rain streaming over her crumpled form. She was only twenty-nine years old, in the prime of her life, and the utter senselessness of the murder filled her family with an unbridled rage. Her brother was filled with remorse for not being home at the time of the break-in; maybe his presence would have deterred the intruder.

———

Krajcir's boldness and deviousness seemed to grow by leaps and bounds as his killing continued. Investigators in four states feverishly sweated over the growing trail of bodies. In addition to Mary and Brenda Parsh, Virginia Lee Witte, Sheila Cole, and Joyce Tharp, there was Myrtle Rupp, a woman found strangled to death with a cord of some kind on April 17, 1979, in her own apartment. Her apartment had been robbed the previous week, and police surmised that the burglar had returned.

A fifty-one-year-old widow, Rupp lived alone in a small apartment in Muhlenberg Township, near South Temple, Pennsylvania. Krajcir had been "Peeping Tomming" in the neighborhood about a week before Myrtle's death. He was peeping into windows and saw her alone in her house on Fifth Avenue. At the time he couldn't break in, so he decided to return later to rape her.

When he came back, he got in through the front door, cut the phone line, and lay in wait for the woman to return home. But when he heard two people talking, he grew alarmed and fled. Unfortunately, very rarely in Krajcir's criminal history did he ever give up on a victim once he'd decided to assault her. He came back to Fifth Avenue a week later, this time armed with a phony badge. He'd purchased the fake police ID at a department store, thinking it was bound to come in handy. It did. When Myrtle answered the door, Krajcir identified himself as a police officer and said he was investigating the burglary that occurred a week ago. She let him in. They talked for a few minutes before he pulled the knife. He forced her to undress in the bedroom and raped her on her own bed. First he used drapery cord to tie her hands and ankles. After the rape, Krajcir used the same cord to strangle the woman to death.

In the spring of 1977, when he was living in the trailer in Carbondale, Krajcir began molesting the adolescent daughter of an acquaintance. She was only eleven years old when the abuse began, and it continued for two years.

It is possible that Krajcir did not think he was abusing her. He may have decided that the two of them had a real relationship going. Decades later, he would refer to the child, who, like an overwhelming majority of sexual abuse victims, remained silent about what she was suffering, as his girlfriend. For two years, Krajcir persisted in forcing intercourse on her, and the confused child said nothing.

In 1979, he got caught. He'd begun abusing the girl's younger sister, and when the girls' mother found out, she alerted the authorities. The allegations led to a search of Krajcir's trailer. Carbondale officers retrieved a small amount of marijuana. They also found a gun. It was a .38-caliber Charter Arms pistol.

Krajcir spent one day in jail before posting bond.

Both girls were bewildered when Krajcir was arrested, confused and upset. The arrest made it seem like he was a bad guy, but neither of them wanted to testify against him. Why they eventually did testify remains uncertain. Authorities may not have given them much choice. Although the girls weren't entirely sure that Krajcir had done anything to hurt them, and he ended up being tried only for the more recent abuse of the younger girl, it was their testimony that put him away for over two years.

Jackson County convicted Timothy Krajcir as a sexual predator. He is believed to have been the first person convicted in that jurisdiction under the civil commitment sexual predator statute, a law that was supposed to keep him behind bars, where he would be provided routine psychiatric care for as long as he appeared to be a threat to society.

Krajcir served his time in Menard Psychiatric Center, where he had the counselors thoroughly fooled. He attended all of the counseling sessions, not only actively participating in but practically leading them. They were designed to provide sexual predators with an understanding of their own actions that, it was hoped, would one day lead to their reforming. Krajcir was probably one of the most enthusiastic participants in these programs.

He helped other inmates face their problems and talk through possible causative factors and solutions. Exhibiting strong leadership qualities and an impressive understanding of the human psyche, Krajcir slowly convinced the therapists that he was capable of rehabilitation. After only a few months, they began to consider him a prime candidate for conditional release. He was enthusiastic and appeared to display a genuine eagerness to understand himself and work through his issues.

Krajcir had always been a student of psychology, and now he read every book on the subject he could get his hands on. During the course of his counseling sessions, his doctors came to the conclusion that he reacted with hostility and anger when he felt the sting of rejection, and then acted out by trying to punish those who made him feel this way. When his feelings of inadequacy were sexual in nature, the anger often pushed him over the edge, therapists determined.

Still, none of the shrinks believed that Krajcir was capable of violence. (In 1979, child molestation was not considered a violent crime.) By 1980, he appeared to have shown so much improvement in the therapy sessions that his counselors were recommending conditional release.

Krajcir did not exhibit an overwhelming number of risk factors for chronic violence, and the doctors determined that the possibility of his committing violent crimes was relatively low. He was able to exercise control over his emotions, they believed, and even when he snapped, and acted out, they believed he went no further than exhibitionism.

The psychiatrists had no idea they were dealing with a man who'd already committed multiple murders and violent rapes. In 1981, they assisted him in applying to the state for a conditional release. The Jackson County state's attorney at the time, John Clemons, fought tooth and nail against it. He knew that Krajcir was a dangerous man. His history revealed someone who was sick and destructive, and Clemons never felt confident that the system had been successful in "fixing" Krajcir in only two years. Under the sexually dangerous person statute, however, the burden of proving that an individual still poses a threat to society falls on the prosecutor. The Jackson County judge believed the psychiatrists who told him that Krajcir was a changed man.

Krajcir walked out of Menard a free man in spring of 1981, complete with a new plan for his future.

He would resume his education and career, working for the Jackson County Ambulance Service, and enroll at Southern Illinois University in Carbondale. He began attending regular counseling for sex offenders at the university, where he talked through his feelings, motives, and urges. Krajcir got a new trailer, away from the little girls he had molested. They never saw him again.

In his criminal justice administration and psych courses, Krajcir was a model student. He knew half the material already from his personal studies and things he'd read in prison. The criminal justice classes focused on basic principles of law enforcement, plus some business management training.

Ironically, at the same time that Krajcir attended these classes, so did the future detective Paul Echols and police chief Carl Kinnison, who were enrolled in the same program. Later, the two men would be instrumental to bringing their former classmate to justice.

Krajcir was also interested in teaching, and accepted a job at Southeast Missouri's junior college as an instructor. He'd be teaching basic nursing classes. Krajcir had accomplished exactly what the prison counselors said he would: he'd become an excellent student, a good EMT, and a productive member of society. On the surface, the recommendation of conditional release seemed to have been the right one.

In reality, it was very very wrong.

Chapter 4

Grover Thompson

SEPTEMBER 7, 1981

Grover Thompson was tired, and his leg hurt. A steady rain pelted the streets of the southern Illinois town of Mount Vernon, soaking his skin through his thin black pullover. The bus station was choked with weary travelers and overexcited kids this time of night.

The severe limp with which he walked may have made him feel self-conscious. As he walked down Broadway, lowering his head against the rain that fell from the gray sky, he absently picked at the scabs on his chin. He'd tried to scrape them off with a pocketknife, but this only made the bleeding worse. His fortunes seemed to be getting worse, too, if that were possible. The red-and-orange-print shirt he'd picked up at a thrift store and kept on his person during warmer weather had ripped a few days ago, and he was using the tattered sleeve to hold up his baggy black pants. Now his wardrobe consisted of the threadbare shirt, a T-shirt, one pair of socks, the black pants, and the black pullover. Fine for Milwaukee, where he'd come from, but not exactly what he needed for the warmer, wetter Mississippi weather he'd see where he was headed. He couldn't remember the last time he'd been able to shower, or wear shoes. The soles of his feet were thick slabs of callused blisters.

Grover Thompson hadn't had an easy time of it, from the very beginning. Being born a black man in the Deep South before *Brown vs. Board of Education* even made the U.S. Supreme Court docket hadn't paved the way for an easy life. The addition of both mental and physical impairments only compounded Grover's troubles. He walked with a limp his whole life, a natural handicap exacerbated by poor medical care.

Grover's two sisters struggled to protect him over the years, but they were working with limited resources themselves. Besides, they had their own lives to manage. If it was difficult for a black man in Mississippi, it was nearly impossible for a single black woman.

Grover was a transient in the truest sense of the word. He'd drifted around the country in search of work for the past several years. That was how he'd found himself in Wisconsin. Grover had hopes of maybe finding some work when he got to Mississippi. Folks in his hometown were friendly to him, for the most part, and might be more willing to take a chance on someone with his shaky work history than strangers he'd encountered in the Midwest. He'd done some manual-labor type of work on neighboring farms back home—mending split-rail fences, keeping the grass cut, that sort of thing. This had given him something to do, and he'd known most of the people who'd hired him.

But the last job he'd had back home had ended badly. The farm sat way out in the country, and the owner, his boss, kept guns. Grover liked the guns, long and smooth, dark cherrywood sliding under his callused fingertips. So much power trembled in his hands, but it wasn't the power to kill. He'd never consider shooting anything, even a coon, and everyone shot coons in Mississippi. No, for Grover, the allure lay in the sound of the shotgun. If he fired that shotgun, everyone would hear it, and they would know it was him shooting it.

Grover had taken the gun from the barn one time. He hadn't even had it in his hands for thirty minutes when people got mad, and officers from the sheriff's department pulled up to the farm, their patrol-car lights flashing and scaring the animals. They told him he had to stop firing the gun. Grover never touched a gun again.

As a young man, he'd lived in Florida for a while, but he'd been arrested several times for trespassing, loitering, and public drunkenness. Grover wasn't sure what triggered it, but at some point he was placed in a psychiatric center and treated for some mental problems they told him he had.

They told him he lived in his own head too much. He didn't grasp other people's motives very well, so he'd long ago stopped paying attention to them. And he didn't always know the difference between real and fake. Schizophrenia, they'd called it; some sort of disorder.

One of the benefits of having been homeless and on

the road for so long was that Grover knew every possible place he could rest. He knew exactly where he could stay and how long he could stay there, how to avoid trouble with the police, and blend in so he wasn't robbed.

And one other thing he knew, one thing every homeless person knew, was that every town had a post office, and every post office was open twenty-four hours a day to everyone. (At least they were in 1981, before the years of tightened security.) Grover just wanted a place to rest, and he wouldn't get a decent snooze at the bus station because of the people hanging out there. Plus, he was desperate to get out of the biting rain.

The lobby of the old post office building was dark, but warm and dry. Grover set down his satchel and lay down on the tile floor, crumpling his T-shirt up in a ball under his head.

As Grover Thompson slept inside the post office, Timothy Krajcir was just finishing up a little act of exhibitionism. He went through this routine maybe seven or eight times a month. He'd just exposed himself to a group of older women as they were leaving the post office. They reacted with the predictable startled shrieks and scandalized giggles. This type of behavior had satisfied him as a sixteen-year-old outcast with no friends. But now he had a job. He had friends. He had his own place. He needed more satisfaction than he got from pulling it out in public.

None of the counseling had ever had any real effect on Krajcir. He had played the part of the reformed sex offender perfectly, but it seemed like he was doing little more than acting. He struggled to appease his cravings with the petty stuff. He would hurt a lot fewer people that way. But even now, with the exposure still fresh in his mind, he felt the white-hot urge to strike. That was when he noticed Ida White. She was an older woman, but in good shape. It was hard to tell just how old she was.

He watched her the whole time she made her way to her basement apartment across the street from the post office. At this point, Krajcir had developed a nearly perfect system for determining whether a woman lived alone, and he was right on target this time.

He'd planned to sexually assault the older woman. When he selected her as a victim, he'd thought she was much younger—she was actually seventy-two years old. Still, that didn't matter to Krajcir as he skulked around the side of her building to the bathroom window.

Clambering through the window of the tiny apartment wasn't difficult for someone of Krajcir's build and athleticism. He'd found it unlocked, luckily, and he dropped to his feet on the floor of the bathroom. Behind the pale shower curtain, Krajcir crouched and waited. When Ida walked into her bathroom and sat down on the toilet, he made his move, lunging at her.

Ida screamed when she saw the hulking figure coming toward her, his large, rough hands grabbing at her clothing. Krajcir hated when women screamed, and would generally beg, threaten, and plead with them to be quiet, but this time he didn't have much leeway. Units in the building were very close together, and it wouldn't take long for the frantic screams of the terrified older woman to alert a neighbor. Besides, the window still gaped open, exposing the primal sounds of panic and fear to people nearby.

The screaming continued for at least a solid minute, the seconds ticking by as Krajcir frantically begged her to stop.

"I won't hurt you if you stop screaming," he repeated over and over in urgent tones.

She had been a feisty old gal, he would remember later, almost fondly. She'd put up one hell of a fight, but eventually he had to shut her up. The persistent screams put an end to any thoughts of doing a sexual assault or robbery. By now, someone would have called the police. Drawing a small buck knife from his jeans, Krajcir punched Ida in the side with the four-inch blade.

He lost track of how many times he stabbed her, but knew he struck her abdomen at least four times before she finally, blessedly, fell silent.

Krajcir had to use his upper-arm strength to lever himself back out the open window. The space wasn't very big, and trying to maneuver his brawny form through the opening while holding himself up took considerable strength and agility. As he was working his way to the corner of the building, the front door to the tiny apartment was flung open.

He'd parked a few blocks away, but he tried to avoid running. Police patrolled the streets of the city fairly aggressively. Mount Vernon's proximity to St. Louis, just on the other side of the river in Jefferson County, gave it a slightly rougher flavor than many southern Illinois towns.

A light rain was falling on the Indian-summer night as Krajcir slid behind the wheel of his car. He stuck to the back roads, avoiding police and looking for somewhere to ditch the knife. About halfway between Mount Vernon and Carbondale, he flung his bloodied T-shirt and the buck knife out the window and as far into a field as he could manage.

Although Krajcir later recalled a clean getaway, Ida White's neighbor Barney Bates told a different story. He said that when he responded to Ida's screams, and barged into her apartment thinking he'd ride to the older woman's rescue, he found Ida battered and bleeding badly from multiple stab wounds, and her attacker still halfway in the window of the bathroom. Bates was a twenty-one-year-old paramedic who knew that Ida lived alone and frequently worried about her well-being. He tried to stop her attacker, remembered a heated confrontation with the man in the window frame. He grabbed at the man's sleeve, grappling for a moment or two, but upon hearing Ida moan in pain, he gave up the fight and let the man flee into the rainy night. The sleeve tore as Bates pulled, and the ripping fabric was the last sound he heard as White's attacker escaped.

Ida White was rushed to a hospital where she remained for several weeks of rehabilitative treatments. As the EMTs prepared her for the trip to the hospital, Bates gave a short, preliminary statement to the responding officer, describing the assailant as a tall, thin black man with facial hair clad in a white T-shirt and jeans. The depiction easily matched Krajcir, whose swarthy complexion occasionally caused him to be mistaken for a non-Caucasian man. After his talk with police, Bates accompanied White to the hospital.

Given the time of Bates's encounter with White's attacker, police figured he could not have gotten far. This just might be an easy crime to wrap up, it seemed. Shortly after the ambulance left, a woman rushed over to an officer who was patrolling the neighborhood. She reported a black man sleeping on the floor of the lobby in the post office.

Less than thirty minutes after Barney crashed through the door of Ida's apartment, officers located Grover Thompson in the post office across the street. He was stretched out on the floor, clothes supporting his head.

When they snapped the cold metal handcuffs over his wrists, Grover couldn't have been more confused. He'd seen the police enter the building, and had fully expected to be kicked out of the post office, maybe even issued a citation and a fine he had no way of making good on.

He was totally unprepared to learn that they thought he'd stabbed someone. They seemed angry, and began going through his things, searching for evidence. One officer took his pocketknife and opened it. There appeared to be dried bloodstains on the blade, they said. They didn't seem convinced by his explanation that he'd used it to pick at the scabs on his face.

The police officers also seemed very interested in Grover's tattered old shirt. When they found him on the floor, he'd been wearing a black pullover shirt and black pants, but he had his red-and-orange-print shirtsleeve tied around his waist to hold up the black pants. The remains of the shirt lay tucked in a ball under his head, along with the rest of his meager wardrobe.

The police hussled Grover into the patrol car, took him to the Mount Vernon Police Department, and placed him in a tiny interrogation room where he stayed while they tried to make contact with Bates. By the time the young paramedic returned from the hospital, the detectives handling the identification could easily have assembled a photo lineup, Grover's attorney later argued. Instead, they chose to escort Bates to a room adjoining the one that held Grover. One detective remarked that they had a suspect they needed him to take a look at.

Every day in the American justice system, prosecuting attorneys use gripping eyewitness accounts and identifications to link defendants to crime scenes. Though many law enforcement officers today realize the flaws inherent in eyewitness identification and photo lineups, attitudes were quite different twenty-five years ago. Eyewitness identifications did, and still do, carry a tremendous amount of weight with juries. After all, if someone saw this person sitting in the defendant's chair commit the crime, watched with their own eyes, and later recognized that individual from a lineup, surely that person must be guilty.

Research studies have shown, however, how easy it is for a police officer, even unintentionally, to influence the outcome of identification. The best way to conduct such identification is to arrange for a double-blind sequential photo lineup, with a police officer who has no involvement in the investigation and no knowledge of who is or isn't considered a suspect. That way, the officer can't either deliberately or accidentally transfer signals through his body language to the witness trying to rely on his or her own memory.

A crucial part of a proper identification procedure involves showing a witness the photos in a sequence, one by one, instead of as an array. Doing so allows the witness to rely on his own memory of the person he saw, and compare it to one person at a time.

Barney Bates peered at Grover Thompson through a one-sided mirror. He could not be certain at first glance that the bedraggled, bewildered black man pacing restlessly around the tiny space was the monster who'd relentlessly stabbed his neighbor in the gut. He remembered the perpetrator as a larger, more hulking type of man; Grover Thompson seemed taller and less muscular.

He had to study the man in the room for quite a while before his features began to look familiar, but the cop told him to take his time. Barney Bates spent a good fifteen minutes watching Grover pace around the room. The time he took to make the identification would be another heavily contested aspect of the procedure used by the Mount Vernon Police Department. Despite his attorney's vigorous objections, Barney's observations would provide the sole evidence that would later send Grover Thompson to prison for the remainder of his life.

At no point during the night did the officers clearly explain to Grover what crime exactly they suspected him of committing, nor did they offer him legal representation. The officers recorded Bates's positive identification, and his word was good enough for them.

Grover spent the night in jail before meeting his court-appointed attorney. Stephen Swofford hadn't been an attorney very long when he received this assignment. Decades later, he would still remember with sadness his client's confusion over why he'd spent the night in jail, and how he'd had to carefully explain the charges.

Swofford recognized a case of improper eyewitness identification when he saw one. The instant he laid eyes on the police report stating that an officer had told Bates they had a suspect they needed him to look at, he knew that he needed to get the identification tossed out for Grover to have a chance in court.

The prosecuting attorney charged Grover with attempted murder. The preliminary hearing featured testimony that Swofford would later use to bolster his contention that his client died in prison an innocent man. An officer testified that Barney Bates had identified Grover Thompson as the man he'd tangled with in Ida White's bathroom, and that it had only taken him about one to two minutes to make the determination.

The identification was enough to convince a judge that a crime had been committed and that Grover Thompson was the man who'd committed it. The attempted murder case was bound over for circuit court based primarily on Bates's testimony.

Stephen Swofford immediately filed a motion requesting that the trial judge suppress the identification of his client. He argued that the identification had been prejudicial and unconstitutional from the start. Grover Thompson had not been informed of his right to have an attorney present. Doing so might have spurred police to use a little more care in handling the identification procedure. Swofford argued that they had had ample time to arrange a photo or even a physical lineup, and did not do so. He further insisted that Bates was informed by the police that Grover was already a suspect, putting the idea in his mind that there were other factors implicating the man, and his identification would just be the final nail in the coffin.

The case went to trial in 1982, and turned out to be a slam dunk. When Ida White took the stand, the jury saw a a sweet-faced old woman who resembled Mayberry's Aunt Bea. By the time of trial, she had been seeing her attacker's face in her nightmares, and it was easy for her to incriminate a black man in the crime since she knew that that was who police had arrested. She said that the man had lain in wait in her bathroom, jumped out, and showed her a small knife. He'd said, "I will kill you and all the white people here," she testified. He then stabbed her in the stomach and all the way around her abdomen, caus-ing extensive injuries. Ida White talked about her terror after the ordeal, the long months she'd spent recovering in the hospital after surgery, and the physical therapy she'd had to go through.

The human memory is extremely complicated, and often works in unpredictable ways. Ida claimed to remem-ber perfectly the threat she said the man uttered, yet was unable to recognize Grover Thompson. Still, her testi-mony was enough to sway a jury.

In actuality, very little physical evidence implicated Grover Thompson. The fabric imprint of a sock was left on the toilet seat in Ida White's apartment. A forensic expert for the state of Illinois testified that the impression did not match that of the dirty white socks worn by Gro-ver the night of his arrest.

Lab tests confirmed that the blood that marred the short blade of Grover's knife was human blood, and pre-DNA-testing capabilities, elementary serology (the study of blood) was all the technicians had to go on. There were no splatters of the kind one might assume would occur as the result of a stabbing. In fact, the amount of blood detected on the knife was so minuscule that it was impossible to determine a blood type. In short, no physical evidence tied Grover Thompson to the attack on Ida White.

Despite Stephen Swofford's efforts to get Barney Bates's identification tossed out, Bates was permitted to testify. His testimony changed at trial, however: according to his initial description, the attacker was a man in jeans and a T-shirt; this time, he said the perpetrator wore a red-and-orange-patterned shirt, exactly like the one found in Grover's possession. He also testified that it took him ten to fifteen minutes to make the identification, much longer than the officer at the suppression hearing had said.

Grover Thompson was convicted of the attempted murder of Ida White. It took the jury only a little over three hours to render its verdict. He received a sentence of forty years, to be served at the Menard Psychiatric Center.

Though Swofford frequently communicated with his client's distraught sisters during the trial and sentencing, he never saw or heard from Grover Thompson or his family after the conviction. The case never stopped plaguing him, however. He was always convinced that the wrong man had gone to prison.

"I'm not the kind of person that takes on causes lightly, but after going through this case I was convinced for years that this man was innocent," Swofford later said.

How could Thompson, a man who could barely walk as a result of his physical handicaps, have possibly made the leap out of Ida White's apartment? Why wasn't there more blood on his pocketknife? And what explained the discrepancy between Bates's descriptions of the clothing White's attacker wore? Not to mention the fact that even Ida White couldn't say for certain who had assaulted her . . .

It's no surprise that the facts of the case continued to disturb Swofford, but there was nothing he could do. Still, every time he saw the investigating officers in the case, or the trial judge, he'd bring it up. He continued to insist that the wrong man had been convicted, and that White's attacker was still at large.

Whenever a rapist or murderer was convicted anywhere within a hundred-mile radius of Mount Vernon, Swofford would wonder if it was the guy, Ida White's real attacker. When DNA testing became more commonplace, Swofford inquired as to the possibility of reexamining the physical evidence. An officer who investigated the case told him he believed all the evidence had been destroyed.

Eventually, Swofford learned that Grover Thompson had died in prison in 1996, after serving fourteen years of his sentence. With his client dead, and no doubt Ida White as well, there was little else he could do. He tried his best to force the troubling case out of his mind.

———

It was a cold night in December of 1981 when Timothy Krajcir attacked in Cape Girardeau for the first time since his parole earlier that year. Grace Larkin* had just gotten home from the store and was sitting on the floor changing a child's diaper. There were six young children, her own and her nieces and nephews, in the house that evening. A frigid blast of night air hit her shoulders unexpectedly as the door swung open and a man with a gun stalked into the room.

The man in the doorway had a blue bandanna masking his face. He demanded money, and when Grace insisted she had none, he asked her to empty her purse. He ordered everyone in the room to lie on their stomach.

Grace intended to fight. She knew her mother had been sexually assaulted when a man broke into her house, and she had no intention of submitting to a similar fate. She knew what that attack had done to her mother. But when the man pointed the gun at her five-year-old nephew, Grace couldn't take the risk that he'd hurt him.

"Where is your sister?" the man in the blue bandanna demanded. Grace's younger, teenage sister was not at home. She told him her brother would be home shortly, and he called her a liar.

Krajcir herded Grace into a room off the front one. He ordered her to remove her clothing and began kissing her skin. She begged him to leave, to just let her and the children alone. He told her she'd either have to have intercourse with him or give him oral sex. He just needed to make up his mind, he said.

Finally he grabbed Grace's head with both hands and

_____
*Denotes pseudonym.

forced himself into her mouth, ordering her to press down. When he ejaculated, he forced her to swallow his semen, telling her she'd better not spill a drop. Then he rushed her to put on her clothes and pushed her out of the room.

After forcing Grace to pull the phone cord out of the wall, he went into the living room and sliced through the phone line there. Grace noticed that the man seemed to know the layout of her house extremely well.

When she described the assault to police, she said her attacker was dark-eyed, with brownish-blond hair, and wore a red plaid shirt with blue or black pants. A blue bandanna shrouded his features. He wore surgical gloves and looked as if he weighed from 140 to 160 pounds.

Cape Girardeau police opened a file on the basis of Grace's report. A psychological profile of her attacker described him as having possible mental health issues in his past and a violent temper. He was someone likely to have been kicked out of school for behavioral or disciplinary problems. Probably he was involved in some sort of contact sports. He might be a heavy drinker, but likely not a drug user.

The profile went on to describe the attacker's personality as volatile, quick to anger, explosive even. He acted on impulse and tended to be self-centered. He was likely to be a loner, and would have made an excellent con artist because he liked to manipulate people. He may have forged transitory, superficial relationships with a few drinking buddies, but didn't have close friendships. His job was probably in construction, something physically oriented, and he was probably from a middle- to lower-class background.

———————

Grace's mother, Francine, never connected what had happened to her daughter with her own assault three years earlier. In July of 1979, she'd been napping on the sofa after a summer's day of gardening when a tall, brown-haired, black-eyed man suddenly appeared. He stood over her slumbering form, brandishing a garden rake she'd left on the porch.

The mother of six, Francine was forty-nine years old at the time. The attacker demanded to know where Francine's sixteen-year-old daughter, Grace's younger sister, was. Luckily, she was babysitting at Grace's house that day.

The attacker, who was, of course, Timothy Krajcir, forced Francine to choose the method he'd use to sexually assault her and threw her brutally to the floor. Fighting had not been an option; he was far too strong. Francine stood less than five feet and weighed only ninety-eight pounds soaking wet.

After he finished molesting her, he ordered her not to move. He cut her phone cord, like he always did. Once he left, she stayed stock-still for a few minutes before making a frantic dash to lock the door. She tried to call for help, but discovered that the phone cord had been severed. She notified police from the house of a relative who lived in the same neighborhood.

Francine spent the night at her son's house, too afraid

to return to the home that should have felt like the safest haven in the world. It didn't, not ever again. When she finally ventured inside the next day, the first thing she did was clean the place from top to bottom.

She never again mentioned the assault to her family. They knew the toll it had taken on her peace of mind, however. In fact, it helped spur Grace's decision to move in with her mother, bringing her three children along. She thought the extra people in the house would comfort her mother. Neither of them ever suspected that the attacker would come back.

JANUARY 9, 1982

Krajcir wasn't a mall person. It was extremely rare for him to prey in such crowded places. He knew he was taking a big chance, parked in such a busy lot, but the West Park Mall had just opened. For a few minutes that night, he genuinely just wanted to check out the new mall in Cape Girardeau, but the urge didn't last long.

When he saw the woman walk out of the mall entrance, he didn't recognize her. It had been four years. Leslie Marcano had her daughter with her again, but she looked so different, so much older. There was no way he could have known. It was just a horrible, terrible coincidence.

As he followed them to their home, he thought the woman looked vaguely familiar, but her looks didn't strike any particular chord with him. He chose not to dwell on it too long. At any rate, the car was different, and he didn't make the connection as he followed her to a relatively new-looking house, and parked a block away.

Leslie had gotten a new house, a new car, and had moved across town. She'd tried to get past the terrifying ordeal of a few short years ago. The neighborhood was nice, mostly apartment complexes and a few small houses like hers.

Krajcir walked around to the small back porch. The January night was frigid, three degrees below zero, and a brutal wind seeped into his bones as he lingered outside the house. He was about half frozen, skulking around behind the little house, and considered just packing it in and driving back to Carbondale. He could turn the heat on in the car, at least. But as he watched, someone finally came into the kitchen. It was Leslie. She carried a bucket and mop, and set to work on the kitchen floor. Krajcir stuck around, watching her hum quietly to herself. This anonymous, unseen intrusion into the private, intimate world of an attractive woman offered him so much. It seemed harmless, but the rush he derived from it was on a par with the experience of raping. Krajcir fingered his gun, a little .25-caliber semiautomatic he'd recently purchased from a coworker.

He knew she'd need to wring out the mop. That was how he got in. The pretty young woman stepped outside, shuddering against the cold, and started to squeeze the soapy water out onto the frozen ground.

"You scared me to death," Leslie said quietly.

She was looking at him as though she recognized him. She'd likely seen this man lurking around every corner and in every dark alley for the past four years, seen him in her mind every time a noise startled her. And now here he was.

He was wearing the same baseball cap he'd had on the first time he'd terrorized her. This time, though, a blue bandanna masked the lower half of his face.

He showed her the gun as he shoved his foot through the door, forcing his way into her house.

Krajcir grabbed Leslie by the mouth a split second too late after she'd screamed and dropped the bucket. Soapy water splashed across the kitchen floor. He made her as much a captive as she'd been in her car. He wielded the gun with as much menace as he had the knife, and gave every indication that he'd use it without any hesitation.

As they walked back inside, Leslie's daughter came running into the room. She'd been in the garage of the small house, playing with her puppy, when she heard her mother's scream, and she started screaming herself.

Krajcir began yelling frantically at the little girl to quit screaming. His tone was hostile and aggressive at first. He repeated the words "stay quiet" or "be quiet" over and over. They went upstairs, the three of them, and Leslie had her daughter lie down on her own bed, face turned toward the wall. She didn't know why Krajcir had selected her daughter's room, but as soon as they got to the top of the stairs, he told her to choose the room to the right.

Leslie wished he'd picked the other room, her own bedroom. She kept a hammer underneath her bed.

After she put her daughter on the bed she covered her up with blankets. She didn't want her to see a thing, not like last time. While she did this, Krajcir wandered into Leslie's bedroom, and she vaguely heard him going through her drawers. When he walked back into the little girl's room, he rummaged through the child's dresser as well.

The scene should have been heart-wrenching. The girl had to watch her mother go through every woman's nightmare, *again,* and Leslie could do little to protect her. Every move the child made seemed to increase Krajcir's agitation and Leslie became desperate to keep her daughter quiet. Although Krajcir soon simmered down slightly, his tone remained harsh and demanding, always with a hint of imminent violence.

"Do what I tell you and I won't have to hurt you," he would say from time to time.

At one point, the little girl began complaining that she was too hot under the blanket. Krajcir suggested that they allow her to watch.

He told Leslie to undress, and tried to shove his penis into her mouth. She quietly told him she would pray for him, that because of her faith, she couldn't do some of the things he was asking. That's when the feeling of déjà vu hit him. She'd told him the same thing the first time, and it had struck him as just as odd then, considering the circumstances.

"You do it and you won't get hurt. You give me any trouble, and the kid will get it and everything else," he said.

Leslie took off her clothes quickly after that.

He started to get a little nervous, and the threats began.
I know where you work.
I know where your daughter goes to school.

I know you moved here recently from down the street.
I've been watching you for weeks.
I know your husband ran out on you.

Each threat he hurled felt like a violent blow, although the part about Leslie's husband was not even true. She'd spent the past four years feeling as though she'd never be safe again, and it turned out she wasn't.

By the time he took off his pants, Krajcir's mood had changed. He became mellower, calmer, seeming to feel like he was in control of the situation. He began asking Leslie the most intrusive questions she'd ever heard.

He wanted to know how long it had been since she'd had sex, and whether she enjoyed receiving oral sex.

Leslie tried to stay noncommittal in her answers. Krajcir had gotten into her home, her daughter's bedroom, her dresser drawers, but he wasn't going to get into her mind.

She told him she didn't know how to do what he was asking, had never given a "blow job," as he phrased it.

"I'll show you what to do, and you just do it," he replied.

She began to gag, and Krajcir grew annoyed. Leslie kept trying to persuade him to go into the other room so her daughter wouldn't have to hear any more—and so that she could get the hammer. But the idea of having the child watching what they were doing excited Krajcir. He promised he wouldn't rape her daughter, but said several times he wanted her to join in so he could "look at her."

Leslie searched frantically for a weapon, something she could readily get into her hands. She pretended to feel sick, and claimed she needed to get to her purse so that she could take her medication. He brought it to her, dumping the pills onto the bed. Then she asked for a drink of water, hoping to sneak into her room to get her hammer. He acquiesced to all of her requests, one after the other, but refused to let her out of his sight.

Eventually, when it was all over, Krajcir told Leslie to lay her head down on the bed, and he went back to peeking through the child's dresser drawers.

Leslie hated having the man behind her, out of her range of vision. She was literally scared to death that he would shoot her and her daughter in the back of the head, though she had no way of knowing he'd done just that to previous victims. She couldn't see the gun. Perhaps she remembered reading about the Parsh killings in the newspaper, and the similarity of the situation struck her.

He tied her and her daughter up, using rawhide bootlaces purchased at Kroger's. He told her he'd only tie them tightly enough so they couldn't follow him, and warned her, again, not to go to the police.

"I won't be back, I won't bother you again," she heard him say as he turned to leave.

As a final insult, Krajcir touched the little girl's butt on his way out of their house, and out of their lives. Leslie fought to stay calm as she got loose and called her brother.

This time, Leslie went to the police and reported the rape. She described Timothy Krajcir as having very muscular legs, a hairy torso, and average build. He wore a dark blue scarf just below short brown hair, masking his face, and on the day he'd accosted her and her daughter the second time, a red-and-white-checkered shirt underneath a jacket.

He must live in the neighborhood, police very quickly reasoned. The rapist seemed to know Leslie, or at least a good deal about her habits. The officer who filed Leslie's complaint noted what a good witness she'd make in court.

"It wasn't a feminine voice, but it wasn't like a husky or deep voice," Leslie told the officer who interviewed her. "It was kind of a soft voice."

Something about Krajcir reminded Leslie vaguely of someone she knew, she told police. She said during the ordeal, she kept thinking to herself, "Could this be him?"

She had an inkling that this was the same monster who had haunted her for the past four years, but she didn't mention this to police. She didn't dare. To have been this man's victim once was bad enough, but to have suffered twice at his hands was too horrible to voice. Two decades would pass before she would make the connection aloud, though she must have mulled over the possibility every day since the attack.

The pain and horror Krajcir instilled in his victims' lives after their paths crossed never went away. Francine gargled with bleach immediately after Krajcir had assaulted her. Grace refused to eat off the same dishes as her family, and briefly turned for solace to alcohol while she struggled with the memory of her assault. She didn't venture out at night alone. Leslie may not have reported her first assault to police, but her daughter never forgot either incident. As an adult, she never felt safe or comfortable in Cape Girardeau, and her mother would always have to travel to visit her, because she wouldn't set foot back in the town.

Chapter 5

Margie Call

With the string of murders under his belt, Krajcir was getting better at pulling off a brutal killing and showing up for his ambulance job the next day, growing ever more convincing at portraying the rehabilitated ex-con. He had a good job, and he was getting a good education, alongside the men who would later struggle fruitlessly to piece together the horrific puzzle he left behind him each time he visited Cape Girardeau.

His approach was practically flawless. He'd venture into a town with which he had virtually no ties. Sure, the Jackson County Ambulance Service made a few stops at Saint Francis and Southeast Missouri, but Krajcir had no family in Cape Girardeau, and no friends there as well. He didn't even have any casual acquaintances or frequent hangouts. Nothing connected him to the town. Krajcir was familiar enough with law enforcement to know that police preferred to work all homicides the same way, even if the crime scene indicated it had been a random act committed by a total stranger. People close to the victim were the first suspects who needed to be ruled out, one by one. And Krajcir only hurt people he didn't know.

Krajcir stayed off the radar. He had lots of friends, and he'd had several girlfriends during the course of his life. Women described him as soft-spoken, intelligent, and charming. None of them could imagine him as someone who would be considered a murder suspect.

He attended every one of his sex offender counseling sessions, just like a model parolee. Back then, he would have had to register in Jackson County as a sex offender, or a "sexually dangerous person," as the state decreed. His counselors were pleased with his pleasant, enthusiastic approach to the sessions. He showed up on time. He made apparent progress by leaps and bounds, just like he'd done in prison. He impressed the counselors with his studies in psychology and his profound understanding of his own actions and motives.

By the time Krajcir killed again in Cape Girardeau, some of the fear and panic he'd left in the wake of killing the Parshes and Sheila Cole had begun to subside. Sheila's father, Harold Cole, continued to venture south every few months and drive the streets of the little riverside town searching for insight into his daughter's senseless death. Floyd Parsh continued to mourn the loss of his wife and daughter, craving justice and answers, but his health was still failing. He remained close with Detective John Brown right up until his death. Brown desperately wanted to give Floyd and Harold the closure they both sought, but he was no closer to resolving the grisly murders than he'd been five years before.

The leads still came in, but their frequency slowed to a trickle. Brown kept the case file on his kitchen table for years. His wife and daughter helped him sort through the myriad leads, interviews, and suspects. Sometimes, he had to remind his daughter that her homework came first, because she would get so caught up in the perplexing cases.

Brown refused to give up on the three 1977 killings. For several years after the slaying of Cole and the two Parsh women, he focused on little else. Sheila's murder had rocked the campus at Southeast, and her sorority in particular. Likewise, the tight-knit neighborhood where the Parshes had lived never totally bounced back. The murders may have faded into the background for most of Cape Girardeau's residents, but the women of Koch Street and the surrounding neighborhood never forgot. They remained haunted by the memory of the two Parsh women and the suffering they'd endured at the hands of the monster with the unknown face. Most people took to locking their doors, something they'd never previously felt was necessary. Even when they were home, they no longer felt safe leaving their houses unsecured.

One woman recalled, decades later, receiving a perverted phone call not long after the murders. The caller asked her intensely personal questions until she hung up, disgusted. The phone call bothered her more than it would have before the death of Mary and Brenda, and it continued to nag her. She clung to the belief that the killer had been the one on the other end of the line. This woman was also close friends with Margie Call.

Everyone in town knew Margie. If you had ever set foot in the Woolworth's store in the Town Plaza Shopping Center, chances were you had exchanged warm conversation and a friendly smile with the charming woman who'd worked there for over thirty years. Margie's world revolved, for the most part, around her loved ones. She was family-oriented, and that family was large and sprawling, located across most of Missouri. Apart from her work and Trinity Lutheran Church, Margie spent most of her time with family and close friends.

Margie's husband, Ernest, had died three years earlier of a heart attack. The postal employee had led a very active life and had been an avid Little League coach.

After her husband's death, Margie surrounded herself with a few close friends and her family. She kept to herself and worked like a fiend. Her boss said she hadn't taken a day off work since at least 1978. Her life slowed down a bit when Ernest died, and she didn't attend her church at all during the month of January. When she went out, it was usually to play cards with her close friends.

Krajcir first spotted Margie at the same place he'd initially laid eyes on Mary Parsh: Kroger's grocery store. He took her to be maybe ten years younger than her actual age of fifty-seven. She stood about five eight, a decent height, and seemed to be in good shape. Her hair was dark, starting to gray, and she wore glasses. Like he'd done with Mary Parsh, he followed the older woman about a week or so before he decided to attack her. He needed to establish that she lived alone before he planned anything elaborate, although he was getting better at picking out his victims. While Krajcir was at Kroger's, he purchased some thin rawhide shoestring. It wasn't expensive, and it was perfect for tying up his victims. The purchase of that cord signified perhaps the most premeditated component of Krajcir's crimes. Ultimately, Kroger's represented the link that would connect most of his victims to one another, though police wouldn't recognize the lead Krajcir had given them for decades.

After scoping out Kroger's, Krajcir followed Margie home to Brink Street. He crept to the back of the ranch-style house and spied on her through the window. She came home alone, confirming his suspicions.

Krajcir returned several days later, around nine on a frigid weekday night at the end of January of 1982. A woman like that, single, conservative, probably early fifties—she wouldn't be the type to stay out past ten in the evening. Krajcir parked the Plymouth he was driving about a block away from the house and walked. He broke in under the cover of darkness. He entered through the same window he'd peeped in a week earlier. This time, he shattered it, just as he'd done at the Parsh home, and accidentally knocked a few bottles off of the windowsill. Krajcir then sat quietly in the living room for twenty minutes, waiting for headlights to cast a glow at the side of the house.

Sometime between nine and nine-thirty, he heard Margie Call's car pull into the carport. He let the woman enter her home and start down the hallway toward her bathroom. Before he had the chance to surprise her, however, she noticed the open window and realized that someone had broken into her home.

She turned and ran. Krajcir hadn't counted on that. It had never happened to him before. No one had ever run on him. He caught her easily, accosting her in the narrow hallway. He led her into the bathroom, guiding her with the same little .25-caliber automatic pistol he'd used to assault Leslie.

He made Margie disrobe, threatening her with the gun. She was terrified; he could see that. He began fondling her until the bathroom with the broken window got so cold that he was forced to move her into the back bedroom.

That was when he tied her up, using the rawhide laces he'd recently purchased. He raped her first. Then he killed her in the back bedroom. Instead of shooting her, as he'd done with his previous victims, he strangled her with his bare hands. First, he stuffed a rolled-up washcloth into her mouth. He placed a pillow over her head before he left. He also sliced off one of her nipples with a small pocketknife. He'd decided that he'd killed enough women to make him a serial killer, and it was about time he kept a souvenir. That was what serial killers were supposed to do, he thought.

He changed his mind about this, though, and before leaving Margie Call's house and vanishing into the night, he flushed her nipple, and the rawhide, down the toilet.

Margie was never late for work. When Woolworth's called her brother Albert Bertling the next morning to inquire about her absence, he knew immediately that something was wrong. Extremely concerned, he left his own job and headed over to Brink Street. When he arrived at Margie's house and found her front door unlocked, Albert's concern grew. There was no way she'd ever have gone to sleep with her door unlatched. Tentatively, fighting back panic, Albert called his sister's name. When he received no answer, he stepped inside.

Albert couldn't see the broken window when he entered, but the house was dead quiet, and alarmingly cold. Perhaps he got the feeling that something very wrong had happened very recently. The first room he checked was the bedroom.

What he saw was his sister's body, lying at the foot of the bed, clothes and belongings haphazardly strewn on the floor. He knew instantly that she was dead, and he didn't approach her body. Margie hadn't even had time to hang up her coat. It lay in a heap by the bedroom doorway. Albert walked straight out to the kitchen and called the Cape Girardeau Police Department.

When two officers arrived, they took note of Margie's nude body, positioned at an angle near the bottom of the bed. She didn't have a stitch on except for a pair of black vinyl boots. A multicolored print blouse lay near her face, and her bra was on the other side of the pillow. The covers on the bed were rumpled. The responding officers left the bedroom, went outside, and called for backup. While outside, one of the officers found a used latex surgical glove near the broken window.

A third officer brought over a borrowed video camera from the department to photograph the crime scene. Police took video footage of the yard and surrounding property before venturing back into the ranch house. While police were combing the house for evidence, an officer retrieved a torn piece of rawhide shoestring in the toilet.

The living room appeared relatively undisturbed. The curtains on both windows were closed, and the television was turned off. Wall-to-wall green carpeting covered the floor, but it was clean, and there were no telling stains. Police searched the room for fingerprints but found nothing.

Margie's bathroom, the scene of the actual attack, appeared relatively clean, aside from the torn string and hair samples retrieved from the toilet. Only a pink throw rug on the floor was askew. Investigators never found the nipple.

One of the other two bedrooms in the house held what police were certain for years was a clue to solving the mystery of Margie's killing. A rose, fashioned of pale yellow silk, lay in the center of the bed. Crumpled tissue paper lay near the flower, and police collected several hair samples from the bedspread, which was neatly tucked in. Investigators felt certain that some significance lay in that yellow rose. The presence of a silk flower resting on the bed of a murder victim was simply too staged an effect to have been just a coincidence. The bed in the second of the bedrooms was slightly rumpled, as if someone had recently lain down on it. An open *Sports Illustrated,* folded as if someone had just been reading an article and been interrupted, had been tossed on the bedspread.

The rawhide found in the bathroom was bagged as evidence, but didn't seem very significant until investigators turned Margie's body over and discovered the ligatures on the bed. They also found the washcloth stuffed in Margie's mouth. There were no visible injuries to her body, except discolorations around her wrists that appeared to be ligature markings. The same marks adorned her neck. Her arms were still stretched backward, indicating that they'd been tied behind her back at some point.

The room appeared disordered, but not ransacked; this led police to believe the killer's motive had not been robbery. Some glass fragments were collected from the bedroom carpet, indicating that when the perpetrator broke through the bathroom window, the bedroom door had been open. Several documents were found under the bed, ripped in half.

That night, then evidence technician Carl Kinnison stayed in the three-bedroom rancher to make sure the killer didn't return and that no one could compromise the crime scene before police finished collecting evidence. He spent most of the night sitting at the kitchen table, listening to the silence and the darkness outside. Margie would have entered her house that night through the kitchen door. It was the one closest to the carport.

The light over the stove cast a soft golden glow over the kitchen. Margie's eyeglasses were still on the kitchen counter. She may have laid them down when she walked in. Her family insisted she would never have retired to bed without her glasses. She kept them close by at all times. She removed them only to go to sleep, and then she always made sure to lay them where she could reach them when she woke up.

Police hadn't been able to detect any footprints from

the three-tone beige floor in the kitchen. A pile of untouched mail and a *Southeast Missourian* newspaper lay on the kitchen table.

It was an eerie feeling for Kinnison, waiting there till the clock ticked into daybreak, to see if the killer was going to return. But someone had to make sure that the crime scene wasn't compromised. Margie's death had sent the town into an immediate tailspin, reevoking the fear that had gripped it after the Parsh slayings.

Interview by interview, police began to trace Margie's last steps on earth, learning she'd worked a full day at Woolworth's and had gotten off around 5 P.M. She'd gone home and flicked on her living-room lights and the light over the carport—she was going back out, and wanted to ensure that she wouldn't be coming home to a dark house. As an older woman living by herself, she'd become very aware of her vulnerability. Her friends described her as quite security-conscious. In fact, Margie Call made a point of always leaving every available light on so as not to walk into a pitch-black house.

A neighbor saw Margie's familiar car pull into her carport around five-fifteen that night. She went through her usual routine of turning on all the lights before leaving a short while later. That evening, Margie had gone to dinner at the home of friends, a married couple who lived nearby.

Neighbors recalled seeing Margie return around nine-thirty, but a half hour later, the carport went dark. One woman distinctly remembered the time because she'd heard a loud bang around the time Margie got home.

She'd glanced out her window just to make sure everything was okay. That was the way things went in that neighborhood. Everyone looked out for one another.

One man who lived a few houses down recalled seeing Margie's living-room light on around six the following morning when he left for work. Another recalled seeing a brown Plymouth parked in front of Margie's residence with the headlights still on.

Four patrol officers were responsible for collecting the rather significant amount of physical evidence Margie's killer had left behind. Of them, three, including Kinnison, would later play integral roles in this case, and in bringing Margie's killer to justice. Officer David Warren retrieved multiple hairs from the victim's bed and body, though years would go by before they could tell him anything, decades before he worked in the crime lab that produced the match to Timothy Krajcir's DNA.

According to a common rule of law enforcement, a homicide offers a very small forty-eight-hour window of opportunity to collect enough evidence to solve a case. The longer a case sits, the thinner the trail of evidence becomes. Witnesses' memories fade, suspects have time to change their stories, and physical evidence disappears.

Aside from Albert Bertling, Margie's brother, who lived in Jackson, a town adjacent to Cape Girardeau, Margie's siblings were deceased or scattered across the country. Her two sons, Gary and Donald, lived in different parts of Illinois. They immediately threw themselves into assisting police with the investigation, finding out as much as they could.

A few days after Margie's death, coroner Harold Cobb called seven citizens to view her body. A coroner's inquest—a practice that dates back to medieval times, when the coroner served the king and a king's jury was impaneled to determine the cause of a death and whether a murder had been committed—is seldom held these days.

An inquest is not a trial, but more of a review of the facts of the case. After this review, the inquest jury provides the prosecution with a recommendation. Cobb didn't request a formal inquest; though a lot of evidence had been gathered, forensic science hadn't progressed to the point where such evidence provided sufficient grounds for an arrest. Besides, police had no suspects to compare anything to. Nevertheless, Cobb wanted to give the jury a look at the body before the autopsy was performed in St. Louis.

Police refused to release many details of the murder to anyone beyond Margie's family and those seven Cape Girardeau residents. They specified only that her hands were bruised as though they had been bound, but she had not been found tied up.

There were no visible puncture wounds, and she had not been shot or stabbed. The public knew that some fingerprints had been found inside Margie's home and were sure that the police would eventually find the killer. Before DNA, fingerprints were all investigators had to go on, but this was more than they'd had with the other murders.

The vast amount of physical evidence recovered was another distinction of Margie's killing, thanks to that phone call Woolworth's made to her brother the following morning. By the time the bodies of Mary and Brenda Parsh had been discovered, the heat inside the un-air-conditioned house had caused any genetic material to deteriorate to the point of uselessness.

After the autopsy, Cobb announced that Margie's death had been due to strangulation, but disclosed little else about the circumstances. Investigators sought to withhold as much as they could so there would be details only the killer could know. For example, the information about the mutilation of the victim's chest—her missing nipple—was not released. Nor were the fresh bruises, indications of rape, found on Margie's inner thighs.

Family members confirmed that nothing had been taken from the house, as far as they could tell. Again, police found themselves in the awkward position of scouring a woman's personal life for something, anything, that would indicate any motive to kill her. And again, they found nothing.

By February 1982 investigators were desperate. They asked for assistance from the Federal Bureau of Investigation. Chief Ray Johnson wanted the experts to draw up a psychological profile of Margie's killer, in the hopes that it would produce some workable lead.

The profile, Johnson hoped, would narrow the scope of the search for the murderer. They had more than enough physical evidence in the case to link a suspect to the crime—if only they could find one. Police still hadn't released the fact that Margie had been raped, but did say that sexual assault was a possible motive they were looking at.

Ray Johnson had been a chief for only a short time

when Margie Call was killed. Just two years previously, he had been public safety director for the town of Des Peres, Missouri, when he'd been faced with a situation every law enforcement agent dreads: four employees gunned down in cold blood. Thankfully, Johnson's department caught and arrested the suspect.

The Margie Call case was different from anything Johnson had experienced. Desperate to quell the rising panic, he immediately began making crime prevention programs a top priority as well as a new 911 system for the Cape Girardeau community. He allocated as many resources as he could to both causes.

As investigators continued relentlessly to toil over the case, Margie's sons, Don and Gary, were racked with guilt; both felt that they ought to have lived closer to her. Don worried about what might happen if the killer was caught. His brother's temper was legendary, and the murder had left them both in a state of rage. For years, Don would have a recurring nightmare that he and Gary were seated in the front row of a large courtroom, looking at the man who'd just been tried for their mother's murder. The man's face was hidden by shadows, and as much as he tried, Don couldn't bring his features into focus. Each time he had the dream, the jury foreman would stand and announce that twelve citizens of Cape Girardeau had found the man guilty. Don would make a frantic grab for his brother, as Gary vaulted over the low barrier separating him from his mother's killer, but would move a fraction of a second too late to stop his brother from lunging at the faceless defendant. He always woke up from the nightmare before he knew whether or not he'd been able to stop Gary from killing the man. He never knew how it ended, and he never knew the identity of the murderer.

At times, it seemed like the killer must've lived in the neighborhood. How else could he have known to strike when poor Floyd Parsh was hospital ridden, or what time Margie would arrive home from her friends' house? Suspicion fell on a pair of quiet, aloof teenagers everyone had seen around the neighborhood. There was never anything to charge them with, but local residents always found them vaguely suspicious, a fact the teens were aware of and angry about.

Margie had scores of grandchildren, nieces, and nephews she'd never get to see grow up. Le Ann, her one granddaughter (the others were all boys), would become a supermodel. All of the children had fond memories of Margie, of her generosity, her cooking, how she'd always have a silver dollar for each child at holidays. Years later, the way his mother had been robbed of her right to be a grandma would weigh on Don's mind. That regret only intensified when his brother and uncle passed away before Margie's killer was brought to justice.

Chapter 6

After Cape Girardeau

APRIL 1982

Until April of 1982, Timothy Krajcir had always made a point of traveling outside of the town where he lived in order to commit his most heinous crimes. Cape Girardeau was a favored hunting ground of his, as was Marion, Illinois. Every murder he committed was far enough away to be untraceable to a convicted sex offender in Carbondale. He typically didn't like hurting people in his own backyard; it's difficult, in retrospect, to understand how he could have rationalized preying on those two little girls, his acquaintances' daughters, although possibly he didn't see them as victims, and didn't think he was physically hurting them.

The only other time Krajcir ever chose to prey on someone close to home, it was really close.

Killing Deborah Sheppard was a crime of opportunity for Krajcir. The bright, attractive young black woman was a marketing major at Southern Illinois University at the time. She was only twenty-three.

Her family lived in Olympia Fields, a village not far from Chicago. Deborah was quite family-oriented, and as the oldest in a family of three girls, she served as something of a surrogate mother to her two younger sisters. She was very responsible. The Sheppard family was huge, with tons of nieces, nephews, and cousins. Though Deborah went to college to study marketing, she'd considered a career in veterinary medicine. Her father, Bernard Sheppard, described his eldest daughter as the type of person to adopt a crippled dog at the pound rather than a healthy one.

———————

It was after dark when Krajcir first spotted Deborah Sheppard. The trailer park where he lived at the time was not far from where the college senior lived. Deborah's apartment was right off the campus, a flat, tan-colored building that comprised several units, and her ground-floor apartment allowed Krajcir to spy on her easily.

It was Easter weekend when Krajcir decided to assault Deborah Sheppard. Her parents and two sisters were planning to visit for the holiday. At the same time that Krajcir prowled the streets of Carbondale looking for a victim, Paul Echols was patrolling the same neighborhood, as a rookie officer for the Carbondale Police Department. It was during Echols's shift that Krajcir surprised Deborah as she stepped out of her shower.

Deborah marked Krajcir's eighth kill. As with Margie Call, he didn't use his gun; instead, after raping her, he strangled her with his bare hands. He then left her nude body lying on the floor of the apartment, the door ajar, which is where she was discovered by a friend.

At 3 A.M. on April 8, Bernard Sheppard received a call informing him that his daughter had been found dead in her apartment. When her family arrived in Carbondale, her father saw the screen that had been removed from one of the apartment's windows, whether by Krajcir or the police, and felt a crushing wave of guilt that he hadn't been on hand to protect his oldest daughter from this monster. Though Krajcir wouldn't become a suspect in the murder for nearly twenty-five years, the knowledge that a stranger had preyed on his daughter would haunt Bernard Sheppard the entire time. He would always lament not having left for Carbondale earlier. If the family had arrived earlier, perhaps they could have prevented the killing.

As with several of Krajcir's murders, the fact that Deborah had been sexually assaulted wasn't apparent right away. Worse, police first ruled that her death had been an accident, and didn't involve any foul play. The first autopsy didn't reveal any bruising or indication that she had been murdered. Her Graham Street apartment had been neat and absent of any signs of a struggle. The place hadn't been ransacked. Unconvinced, the Sheppard family paid to have Deborah's body flown to Cook County, Illinois, where the county medical examiner performed a second autopsy. This time, physical evidence that she'd suffered two sharp blows to the head was found. The medical examiner also ruled that there was enough evidence to indicate that Deborah had died by asphyxiation or strangulation, either smothered with something or choked. The death was now marked a homicide.

Police couldn't link Sheppard's death to an ex-boyfriend or anyone with a personal motive. They searched all databases for the names of convicted killers living in the area or within a hundred-mile radius. Police had their suspects, as they'd had with the other murders, but were never able to find anything concrete. Nothing traced back to Krajcir.

———————

Krajcir made several trips to Cape Girardeau in 1982, the same year he killed Deborah Sheppard and Margie Call. On one of these jaunts, in late April, he came across a house where three women in their twenties, three friends, had gathered with their children for the evening. He'd spied one of the women, an attractive young black woman named Carol Kirchner,* at a grocery store earlier that week.

When he'd been in prison, Krajcir had had a recurring fantasy he'd always wanted to act out. He'd dreamed about sexually assaulting multiple women at the same time. With the Parshes, though his original target had been Mary, he'd focused primarily on her daughter Brenda. When he'd seen Carol in the store and followed her home, he hadn't known his dreamed-of opportunity would be presenting itself a few days later, on the night he chose to return to her house.

On April 25, 1982, Carol and two friends, Gretchen Lockwood,* and Dorothy Quay,* decided to get together at Carol's house on Hanover Street. A hen party, they called

———————

*Denotes pseudonym.

it later, full of gossip and cocktails. Carol was then twenty-eight, Gretchen was twenty-four, and Dorothy was twenty-seven. The three women had been friends since adolescence, and had spent many weekends together, hanging out, laughing, and talking.

Krajcir cut through a screen on the back door to get in and crept through the house while the women caught up with one another. Carol and Dorothy's children were playing in the back of the house, and he must have herded the children in front of him, because the first thing the women saw when they looked up were two of the kids scampering into the room.

Behind them stood a man brandishing a pointed gun. He aimed it straight at the children as they lined up quietly in front of him. The man had a dark blue sock cap pulled down over bushy eyebrows and a blue bandanna tied around the lower half of his face, masking his features like some kind of Wild West bandit. It was between nine and ten in the evening when the terrifying intrusion interrupted their conversation.

All eyes focused on the gun in his hand. A black rubber glove encased his other hand, but no one in that living room noticed it right away.

"This is not a play gun," he said. His voice was soft. He must have known how surreal the situation must have seemed to the women, and that all three of them were thinking that the small black pistol *looked* like a toy. The man stalked toward the three petrified women, ordering them to lie facedown on the floor.

He forced all of the younger children in the house into a closet and turned off the light so they wouldn't be able to see what was going on. He held the gun trained on the children as he moved, knowing it was the best way to keep the adults in line.

He made the women do unspeakable things in that room. Pointing the gun, he ordered Carol to undress and turn completely around in circles so he could look at her. After he finished ogling her, he instructed her to sit down on him and grind back and forth. Then he made her give him oral sex while he roughly fondled one of her friends.

He made Carol walk over to the sofa and bend over nude, and he watched her while continuing to fondle her friend. He forced the third female to undress while he abused the first two. Eventually, Krajcir demanded that all three of his victims bend over the sofa, nude, while he caressed and kissed their bodies. He made them dance for him as he sipped from their margarita glasses. At one point he sexually abused Dorothy, using the gun. It was horrible for the women to have to watch their friends being so brutalized. As long as he wielded that black gun, his control over them was absolute. During the assault, they prayed, and cried, and frantically sought escape from the horror of the situation they'd found themselves in. Carol said she was going to throw up.

"I want you to do whatever I tell you to do, or I'll beat the kids up the side of the head," he told the women. Looking at those dark eyes and what little of his face was exposed, they believed him.

He went back to forcing himself on Carol, and this time ejaculated into her mouth. She spit out his semen on the back of the sofa.

Then he robbed them.

"Where is your purse?" he asked them in turn, allowing each woman to retrieve her purse and then instructing her to empty it. They had to dump out the contents onto the floor as he rifled through their belongings and took what he wanted. "All I want is money," he kept saying, though he ended up taking their jewelry, too.

Before he made a quiet exit, Krajcir checked on the children in the closet, saying he wanted to make sure they were all right. He told the three traumatized women that he'd know if they stood up because he'd hear them. They needed to lie still and wait for five minutes before getting up, he said. They waited for ten minutes, then one of the women hurried to the kitchen and shut the door. He'd left it wide open, with the three of them still undressed, and a chilly early spring breeze blowing in.

Once they were certain their tormentor had really left, they freed the children, hugging them fiercely. Carol had no phone at the time, so Dorothy had to drive to her house to call the police department and report the assault.

All three women described Krajcir as standing about five eight, around 160 to 170 pounds, and dressed in a blue sock cap, with a bandanna tied around his face. He had on blue tennis shoes, jeans, and a denim jacket. All three women described him as having dark, bushy eyebrows, piercing black eyes, and a soft voice. He had at that time a rather bushy mustache that all three victims described as his most noticeable feature, which was just visible above the bandanna.

They reported that the intruder had entered the house, threatened them at gunpoint, forced them to perform indecent acts, and taken some cash from their purses. They thought he'd taken off in a northerly direction, toward the center of town.

A few days later, the women were asked to view a lineup, but none of the men they saw matched their memories of their assailant. The story sounded so incredible, so unbelievable, they worried that the police wouldn't take it seriously.

That one night of terror forever changed their lives. Dorothy had been married for only two weeks when Krajcir attacked her. The marriage didn't last through the year, and she believed the assault was the reason. She moved across the state, trying to escape the memories of what had happened in Cape Girardeau. For years after that, she would tie a string to her doorknob as a way of knowing whether or not anyone had entered her home before her, and she kept a baseball bat in bed with her.

Carol went to bed every night with her sofa pushed flush up against the door to the house so intruders would have one more obstacle barring their entry. Just in case, she also slept with a meat cleaver and put a hammer beneath her bed.

MAY 17, 1982

Elza Seabaugh was dozing quietly in his lounge chair, drifting off to the strains of gospel music, when he heard his wife, Eunice, scream. It was shortly after nine in the evening of Elza's seventy-ninth birthday. Eunice had just finished straightening up their record collection. She'd settled down on the floor and leaned back when a pair of dark-colored shoes and pants appeared in her line of vision as she glanced toward the door. The intruder's approach had been so silent that Eunice hadn't even noticed it until he was close enough to reach out and touch her. He took about five more steps into the room. She gave a short scream.

Waking with a start, Elza saw a large man step in front of him, blocking Elza's view of his own television set. Here, inside their small but comfy home on Middle Street in Cape Girardeau.

"I want your wallet," the man said.

Refusing to be robbed in his own home, on his birthday, Elza said the first word that came to his mind. "No."

"I'll shoot you if you don't give me your wallet," Krajcir told him.

Reaching into his pocket, Elza drew out a pocketknife.

He threatened to cut the intruder's throat. As he flipped open the knife, his movement was shaky and he accidentally sliced into his own skin.

Again, Krajcir threatened to shoot him if he didn't turn over his wallet. Through the entire altercation, Krajcir remained as cold as ice. He didn't budge an inch, or react to Elza's threats, even when the older man put all the resolve he could muster into his voice.

"You'll have to shoot me, then, because I'm not giving you my wallet," he said, trying to sound firm.

Krajcir turned the gun on Eunice, training it on her.

"I'll shoot her," he said, his voice soft.

Eunice quickly grabbed her husband and pulled him down to her level.

Again Krajcir demanded Elza's wallet, and again the man refused, insisting that the robber would have to shoot him first.

Not willing to risk her husband's life for his stubborn pride, Eunice finally grabbed his wallet, jerking it free from his pocket and flinging it at their assailant.

Krajcir removed the cash and threw the wallet back at the couple, as though the delay caused by the man's stubbornness had irritated him. He then ordered them to lie down on the floor while he had a look around. He said he would be about five minutes.

He asked the couple how many phones they had, and whether or not they had any more money. Eunice provided the answers while her husband shook with fury on the floor beside her. She convinced Krajcir they had no more cash in the house. Krajcir said he would cut their phone line. He said he wanted their faces pressed to the floor, and if they moved, he would shoot. Eunice believed his threats.

"I don't want to hurt nobody. I just want your money. I'll take it and leave," he finally said quietly, turning to go.

Elza Seabaugh jumped to his feet and went for his gun as soon as Krajcir was out of sight. He couldn't lie there waiting while this armed intruder prowled around their house, rifling through their personal items. He turned on the porch light. Krajcir appeared in a wash of light, near the porch, both hands on his gun. The short barrel stuck out about an inch or two from his hands. Elza didn't shoot, but he got a good look at their assailant as he made his escape.

The gun was black, with some white enameling around the barrel. The man wore dark clothes, and didn't appear to be very old. He had a dark complexion, not Caucasian. When he talked, his voice was soft, almost kind-sounding. He had a very clear and precise manner of speaking that struck both Eunice and her husband. It was obvious that he was not uneducated.

For the rest of his life, Elza lived with the knowledge that he'd allowed this intruder to steal from his wife and him in their own home and threaten his wife of forty years. He never recovered from the feelings of vulnerability and helplessness he'd felt that might. Like many Missourians, Elza owned a gun. He never thought something like this could happen to him, not to his family.

In 1982, as mentioned earlier, Missouri was a Castle Doctrine state, as it had been for for eight decades, by case law if not actually on the books. This meant that all residents of the state had the right to use deadly force when an intruder broke into their home and threatened them or their belongings. They needed to have a reasonable belief that the person was trying to hurt or rob them, but in such cases, deadly force was considered a justifiable or excusable reaction by the courts. It wasn't unusual for Missourians to keep guns in their houses in the event of a break-in, never expecting to have to use them.

After their experience with Krajcir, the Seabaughs realized that maybe owning a gun wasn't a sufficient deterrent. They erected a six-foot fence around the yard, determined that no one would ever enter their home uninvited again. They acquired two big dogs to guard their residence as well.

Eunice thanked God for years that the man with the soft voice, awful as he had been, had not harmed them. The Seabaughs were lucky: a month later, the man who had broken into their home killed his next victim.

It would be Krajcir's ninth murder victim, though he had tormented countless others. Twenty years would pass before police could even count the number of Krajcir's murders. When they did, his other crimes, those that had left the victims alive but never the same, would again surface, bringing closure along with fresh pain. These victims at last knew the identity of their tormentor. In learning it, they also had to realize they could easily have been among those he had killed.

JUNE 20, 1982

It was almost like clockwork at this point. Krajcir moved briskly down the darkened pavement. He was well aware that the constant flow of traffic on William Street, a main thoroughfare of Cape Girardeau, would conceal his forced entry. Still, he remained alert, his senses heightened.

He didn't really know what he was going to end up doing to the woman he'd spotted earlier that day in Kroger's. The neighborhood grocery was rapidly turning out to be his favorite hunting ground, though he still frequented the Wal-Mart, farther along William Street, on the fringes of town.

Krajcir remembered Mildred as an attractive woman,

more handsome than pretty, very fit and slender. She wore her sandy-colored hair short, neatly trimmed to above her ears, and dressed well, like she had some professional job. He thought that she looked to be around forty-five; he'd have been stunned to learn she was actually sixty-five. When he saw her walk to her car, he didn't even have to think. The desire to follow her home, see if she lived alone, had been instinctive.

His intentions wouldn't become clear, even to himself, until he came face-to-face with her. He'd probably do a sexual assault of some kind, but it was too early to tell what kind it would be. He hadn't meant to brutalize the last murder victim, Margie Call, the way he had. That one had gone terribly wrong. She'd run, and he'd known he could very easily have gotten caught. He hadn't even retained the little souvenir he'd taken during the killing. It had been so senseless, such a waste.

Krajcir parked about a block and a half away from the small carport where the woman's car stopped—not far from where Margie Call had lived—and walked the rest of the way. Hanging back slightly, he peeked in through a window and saw the woman pacing restlessly through her house. She seemed to be looking for something, and at some point decided she needed to step out.

Krajcir wasn't going to wait around for her to catch him prowling around outside. He acted quickly, seizing the opportunity to break in while she was gone. He'd seen all he needed to see. The woman lived by herself. There would be no boyfriend or husband to interrupt them.

Creeping around to the west side of the residence, dark blue bandanna tied securely around the lower half of his face, Krajcir approached the small window he guessed led to the woman's bathroom. It was placed a little high for his liking, but that didn't mean it wasn't accessible.

Waiting for the right moment, he prepared himself to sprint if anyone in the aluminum-sided house next door noticed him lurking in the shadows. The light on Pacific Street flashed green and several cars rolled by. Taking care to stay out of the soft glow of headlights, Krajcir selected a rock and threw it at the glass window.

The glass shattered with a satisfying crack and he lightly pushed the pane inward, cringing at the light tinkling of glass shards hitting the ceramic tile of the bathroom floor on the other side. Everything on the windowsill ended up on the ground outside—makeup case, pill bottles, and a razor kit. Krajcir ignored it. It took a few tries to hoist himself up by the arms, but on the third go he gained enough leverage to get his feet under him.

He landed lightly on the other side, in the scramble slicing his left hand on a glass shard on the window frame. Rivulets of blood trickled off his hand, splashing onto the tiled floor.

Luckily, the woman kept first-aid supplies in the cabinet in the small bathroom. Krajcir pulled a Band-Aid from its box on the shelf and used it to stop the bleeding, but not before a few more drops of blood fell to the floor. Krajcir carelessly dropped the Band-Aid wrappers to the ground. Taking a look around the house, he saw a chair strategically placed near the door to block anyone from entering. It hadn't been very effective. That bathroom window had been easy as anything to break.

While he waited he took a bottle of orange juice from the fridge and drank it, keeping an eye on the window in one of the bedrooms for the woman's return.

He heard her car and saw the lights of her powder-blue Mercury Montego sedan flick off. When she entered the small house, he heard her switch on the small television set in the kitchen, put on what sounded like the evening news. She set something wrapped in plastic down on the counter, and he heard the metallic tinkle of her keys landing beside it. At that point, she had no reason to suspect that anything was wrong.

Krajcir quietly lay in wait for her to approach the end of the hallway. He stayed in the back room, which contained a typewriter. The woman had begun to undress for bed at the same time as Krajcir stepped toward the bedroom, stalking down the hallway with his gun drawn. It was a .38 Smith & Wesson pistol, and he waved it as he threatened her with violence.

If Mildred was scared, she refused to show it. In fact, she reacted to the intruder with dignity.

She quietly asked him, point-blank, if he was the one who had killed Margie Call. He hadn't known the other woman's name any more than he knew Mildred's, but he knew she meant the woman on Brink Street. He denied it, knowing otherwise that he'd have to kill this woman, too, which wasn't part of his plans for the night.

Krajcir forced her to finish taking her clothing off, but he didn't let her remove everything. She had stripped down to her waist so that her red dress was still partially covering her body. Mildred Wallace didn't cry. Sitting in the middle of the bed, despite her nudity and the sheer horror of the situation, she folded her legs under herself defensively. Krajcir bound her wrists tightly behind her back with rawhide cord. He also blindfolded her.

He began raping her in the facedown position, but stopped the attack when she complained he was hurting her. It wasn't the first time Krajcir changed his plans in an apparent effort to accommodate the victim; he'd done the same thing with Leslie in the car the first time he'd assaulted her. It was almost as though he liked to pretend the women were enjoying what was happening. At such moments Krajcir tended to disappear into his own mind. He'd been careful, he'd done everything by the book, and all he had to do now was finish the job and get out without being caught. The act of raping a woman usually unleashed memories of every woman he'd ever attacked, and sparked fantasies about the ones he hadn't.

He stopped having intercourse with Mildred, but forced oral sex on her, and she didn't protest. She was near the foot of her bed during the rape, but after he climaxed, he rolled her to the side, closer to the edge. He cut the phone cord, thinking she would be unable to call for help. Then, for reasons he wouldn't be able to articulate, he changed his mind about leaving her alive.

In all honesty, there was no good reason for Krajcir to kill this woman. She hadn't struggled, and he'd kept his bandanna on the whole time. She hadn't seen his face, and he'd denied her accusations about his other victim a few months earlier. None of this mattered in the heat of the moment, however, and years later, Krajcir would be unable to say for certain why he'd done it. He walked straight back into the bedroom once he'd made up his mind, though, and there was no going back. He looked at the woman lying on the bed and shot her point-blank in the head.

Execution style—that was what the authorities would call it, Krajcir thought to himself as he stuffed the gun into the waistband of his jeans, tugging his T-shirt over the bulge. Police would no doubt read some sort of significance into the blindfold and the bound hands, even if there was none. That was better for Krajcir; it would make him more difficult to find. Let them chase their own tails awhile.

He removed some cash from Mildred's purse before leaving the house, then threw a beige towel over the wooden window ledge in the bathroom, leaving the way he came. This time, the glass bits didn't bite into the back of his thighs as he rested in the window frame before lightly leaping to the grass below. Not a soul was in sight on Hanover Avenue as he made his way down toward Good Hope Street, which he knew would be desolate at this hour. One glance over his shoulder revealed a dark and quiet white house, one up from the corner. From here, the broken window was concealed to everyone except the mosquitoes that had likely discovered it by now. Nothing betrayed the sight that would greet anyone who ventured inside the orderly little home. With each step, the dead woman became more of a memory, a fantasy he would switch his mind back to whenever he chose. He didn't give her another thought as he drove across the state line, leaving Cape Girardeau in his tail-lights.

———————

Dawn broke over the Mississippi River just as it did any other day. The mercury sat at about seventy-six degrees, with a bright, clear sky overhead and a light breeze. Warm, stale air wafted into Mildred Wallace's house. College students jogged by, a few roller-skated, taking advantage of the warm temperatures. In a few hours, the sun would blister the pavement.

When Marquette Cement, where Mildred worked as an office manager, called Jean Orsina, Mildred's niece, and Bernice Mercer, Mildred's sister and Jean's mother, to say that Mildred hadn't yet called or shown up for work, they were worried. Mildred's family hadn't heard from her since the night before.

Bernice's worst fear was that her sister might have fallen too ill to call in sick. Though her energy and good physical shape often fooled people, Mildred *was* sixty-five. There was legitimate cause to worry. After all, the coworker who had called told Bernice she couldn't remember a time when Mildred had been even fifteen minutes late, let alone over an hour. She wasn't answering her phone, and she hadn't called in sick or let Marquette know she wouldn't be coming in.

Mildred Wallace had lived in the same house on William Street for eighteen years. She'd never married, and she hadn't been sexually active at the time of her death. She had no boyfriends nor was she dating anyone as far as her family knew.

Mildred had managed the office of Marquette Cement Company for about thirty-five years. She was active in civic organizations and friends called her a workaholic. A conservative dresser, she tended to live frugally, although she was well-off. She didn't drink or smoke. She watched the news at ten every weeknight as part of her routine.

The night of her murder, Mildred had left her sister's house around ten; her second trip because she'd returned to pick up a piece of cake she'd forgotten. That was the last time her sister, her niece Jean, and Jean's three-year-old daughter saw her alive.

As Bernice pulled alongside Mildred's little white house, her daughter and granddaughter with her in the car, she saw her sister's car parked in its usual spot. For the umpteenth time, she wished her stubborn sister had been persuaded to take a roommate, but she knew how fiercely Mildred cherished her independence. Shaking her head, she jogged toward the front door. Had her gaze been drawn to the left, she would have noticed the bathroom curtain fluttering in the soft June breeze, seen the jagged bits of glass clinging to the wood and the towel still draped over the frame. Bernice rapped hard on the aluminum screen door. She heard no welcome sound of footsteps. Smelled no coffee brewing. If there was no coffee, it meant Mildred wasn't awake yet. Bernice did hear noise, but it sounded like the small television set in the kitchen. Fear knotted in her stomach at the notion that something could be really wrong with her sister.

After retrieving the key she knew her sister tucked under the welcome mat, Bernice tugged at the aluminum storm door in the front of the house. She cursed under her breath as she found it locked. Picking up a rock from the side of the driveway, she hammered at the thin glass pane till it broke. Using the spare key, she frantically unlocked the door and burst into the house, calling for Mildred.

No answer.

The kitchen was clean, as neat and orderly as she'd ever seen it. The stainless-steel sink glistened, not a dirty dish in sight. Bernice registered this, somewhere in the back of her panic-stricken mind, as she ran through the house to her sister's bedroom.

She didn't look at the bed, not right away. Her eyes darted to every other conceivable space in the room first as she paused in the doorway, as though her subconscious mind knew what she would find. By the time her eyes fell on the bed, the sight of her sister's naked body, propped up in bed, blindfolded, partially covered by bedclothes stained dark with blood, was almost anticlimactic.

Jean, who followed her mother inside, said she bent over and touched her aunt's face, and her skin felt cold and clammy. The women were horror-stricken. They went to call for help and found the end of the phone cord dangling uselessly where it had been severed from the wall. They had to leave Mildred's house to call the police.

———

Cape Girardeau detective John Brown arrived at the scene shortly after nine that morning. When he got there, the outside of the little white house and surrounding lot were already being videotaped by other officers. Still photographs for evidence were taken with both normal and wide-angle lenses and color-print film.

Mildred Wallace had been security-conscious, just as Margie Call had been. She was a Neighborhood Watch leader. She knew the importance of home security, and had sufficient outdoor lighting, though it had been off that night. Her light blue sedan still sat in the carport, all the doors locked.

The place where the killer had gained entry was obvious. Everyone saw the shattered window, the toiletries scattered underneath it. Closer examination of the glass still sticking to the frame confirmed that the window had been broken from the outside.

Brown had a patrol officer stand guard at the kitchen door while he perused the house, making sure no one entered and maintaining the integrity of the apparent crime scene. He did a quick once-over of the house himself before other officers arrived to assist with the evidence collection. The lights in the kitchen were turned off, and Mildred had had time to set the piece of carrot cake she'd taken from her sister's house on the counter. Her car keys lay next to it. The dishes were clean and stacked up in the sink. A bottle of orange juice was apparently missing from the fridge, since the cap was on the counter. The bottle was later found in the bedroom, near the window. Police surmised the killer may have taken the juice out of the fridge and drunk from the bottle as he watched through the window, waiting for the victim to come home. The kitchen door was locked, dead bolt slid carefully into place. Mildred Wallace had either surprised her intruder after he was already inside her house, or she'd been at home when he broke in. A chair had been used to block the door for added security, but it had been moved to the side.

The houses on that end of William Street were relatively close together. The victim's own white one-story sat exactly eleven feet from the next house. How was it possible, wondered Cape Girardeau chief Ray Johnson, that so brutal a crime could have gone down in such close proximity to neighbors, on a busy city street, and no one noticed the intruder skulking around the house?

Another older woman living by herself, Johnson thought. On the surface, that was enough of a connection for investigators to grab hold of, but he knew there was more to it. The latest victim's house had been in the same relatively nice middle-class neighborhood as that of the Call woman, killed in January. The killer didn't stumble upon these victims by accident. He stalked them. He knew they'd be alone, either because he was someone close to the women, or because he'd been watching them.

As a police officer, Johnson preferred to think that the slayings were not random. Most homicides are committed by someone close to the victim. The rule is especially true with women. Pointing the finger at a jilted lover or an estranged spouse would have a neat and tidy solution. Too much didn't add up, however. The chances of two women being murdered in the same neighborhood seven months apart, both raped and brutalized in their own homes, was too glaring a coincidence.

In both cases, the killer had gained entry by shattering a bathroom window. The killings occurred before midnight, an unusual time for such a bold crime. Homicides tended to occur in the wee morning hours, after the bars closed and the streets were deserted. At 10 P.M. there was still a moderate amount of both car and foot traffic on the streets. The odds of two killers taking this kind of a risk were slim. And then there were the hands, bound, both times, just like the mother and daughter on Koch Street. There, the perpetrator had used cable from the television, but in both this and the Call slaying, the women's hands had been bound tightly with what appeared to be shoelaces. If the women had been given the opportunity, they might have been able to escape.

No, as badly as Johnson wanted to think that these had been personal killings, deep down he knew he was dealing with something else entirely.

———————

The body had been severely brutalized. Mildred's red terry-cloth dress was pulled up to her chest, leaving her mostly nude on the still made bed. Her feet were bare. She lay on her back across the bed. A pink nightgown was wrapped around her neck. Dried blood had coagulated on her thighs and buttocks. Blood had poured out of her ears onto the blindfold.

A pool of blood cushioned the spot on the bedspread where her head rested. Brown-and-gold nylon laces bound her hands. The blindfold was made of a blue strip of terry cloth. Both entry and exit wounds were readily visible on Mildred's head, and the spent bullet lay about three and a half feet from her body. It had pierced through the right side of her temple. The bedroom was orderly and did not look as though anyone had ransacked it. The only evidence of a burglary or home invasion lay in the white purse, its items covered in blood splatters and dumped out on the bedroom floor. The ceiling light had stayed on all night, and the closet in the room appeared undisturbed. Robbery did not appear to have been the predator's sole motive, because the house had not been ransacked thoroughly, although some cash was missing.

The bedroom farther down the hall had several drawers left open in the dresser. Mildred had had time to remove several pieces of jewelry before she'd been attacked. They lay strewn about the room, leaving police to believe the intruder may have surprised her as she was disrobing.

The bathroom lay in shambles, more so than any other room in the house. Glass fragments were scattered all over the floor. Police were able to gather hair and blood samples from the floor and the inside of the closet. It looked as though the intruder may have cut himself breaking in and dripped blood all over the floor. Some Band-Aid wrappers were found on the floor as well.

In 1982, forensic science was totally different from today. Blood evidence was always preserved as best as possible and crime labs could do a lot with latent fingerprinting, but for the most part, a lot of it was still guesswork. A crime scene couldn't be taken apart and put back together the way crime labs are capable of doing today, although shows like *CSI* lead the public to overestimate what can usually be discovered. The best technicians could do with blood samples was take the blood type, and do some basic serology tests if the quality of the sample was really good, looking for certain characteristics that could then be compared to a known sample from the victim or from a suspect.

The blood found in the bathroom turned out to be a positive. It also turned out to match samples taken from the Margie Call homicide, providing the first solid link between the two murders. Further comparison testing on the blood, however, did not match.

Usable latent fingerprints were found on the bathroom window and the living-room wall. The strongest piece of physical evidence police had to go on was a palm print, found on the outside north wall of the residence. It looked as though the perpetrator had been leaning on the building peering inside at the victim. The evidence was sent all over the state, but to no avail. The bullet turned out to be a .38-caliber, 125-grain Winchester semijacketed hollow-point round, likely fired from a Smith & Wesson revolver.

Bullet analysis is part of a field called tool-mark examination, or the study of the unique markings left behind on certain weapons. When a bullet is expelled from a gun, the inside of the chamber leaves rifling impressions on its surface, essentially fingerprinting it. While not 100 percent accurate, study of the markings can often lead to identifying a specific manufacturer of a firearm.

Tool-mark experts can narrow down the potential gun manufacturers by entering the characteristics of the rifling impressions into a database. The database, updated yearly, spits out a list of manufacturers that produce guns with chambers capable of producing those markings. In

1977, police were able to determine that the gun used to kill Mary and Brenda Parsh, and later Sheila Cole, was likely the same weapon—a Charter Arms pistol. In Mildred Wallace's killing, they determined the likely gun came from Smith & Wesson, and again, they were right.

A shoe print was also found near the bottle of orange juice. Further analysis revealed that the print came from a tennis shoe, possibly a Sears brand.

Traces of sperm were found on the bedspread of the victim's bed, though friends and family insisted that Mildred had not been sexually active. The autopsy didn't confirm whether or not she had been sexually assaulted, as the only semen evidence was found on the bed, not on her body. Sexual assaults are sometimes difficult to determine postmortem. Her body had not been mutilated like that of Margie Call, but certain aspects of the murder, such as the blindfold, indicated a possible sexual motive.

Cape Girardeau police contacted the Federal Bureau of Investigation for help with profiling the killer. The physical evidence in the case was entered into the FBI's services, where a suspect profile was created. The file was broken down into three sections: one to catalog possible suspects in the case, an evidence list containing all of the lab reports, and an investigation component containing all other details, including victim information.

With Mildred's death, full-blown panic erupted in the town of Cape Girardeau. Applications for gun permits spiked over 70 percent. To ease some of the tension, Detective Lieutenant John Brown organized a meeting of Mildred's women's group. He spoke with the women candidly, though he left out details about Mildred's suspected sexual assault. He offered advice on how they could protect themselves from the killer.

Cape Girardeau no longer felt safe to its residents. Not only were people who had always left their doors and windows unlocked now bolting their houses up tightly, but women were beginning to carry guns. One woman said she took to sleeping with a Louisville Slugger under her bed. Another mentioned sleeping with a butcher's knife under the pillow.

The major case squad was formed in 1983, shortly after the murder of Mildred Wallace, Krajcir's most recent Cape Girardeau victim. John Brown was one of the original members. The level of fear in the city was at an all-time high, especially among women, but also men who were reluctant to leave their mothers, wives, and sisters home alone if they worked nights. The squad was formed to combat any new murder by establishing a saturation investigation right off the bat, dispatching a swarm of the most experienced and skilled detectives from the Missouri State Highway Patrol, the Cape Girardeau Police Department, the Federal Bureau of Investigation, and the Cape Girardeau County Sheriff's Department. A few years later, nearby rural Bollinger County joined forces and assigned several sheriff's deputies to the case squad. Working off the premise that most homicides must be solved within the first forty-eight hours to have a prayer of catching up with the killer, the squad would eventually have a near-flawless record, with only two unsolved cases to its name by 2008.

Brown had been devoting the majority of his time at

the Cape Girardeau Police Department to working the Krajcir cases, before the formation of the case squad, but with it now up and running, he had new options through which he could carry out his investigation.

Chapter 7

Caught

In the end, it was nothing more than a parole violation that put a stop to Timothy Krajcir's reign of terror. He never transferred his parole-conditioned release to his home state of Pennsylvania, but in late 1982, he moved back to the Lehigh Valley. He never notified his counselors or his parole officer of his departure. He never went through he proper legal channels, never transferred any of the parole paperwork form state to state. By Illinois law, this gave authorities the right to yank his parole and throw him straight back in Menard Psychiatric. Eventually, they caught up with him.

Almost immediately upon his return to Pennsylvania, he began terrorizing women.

He robbed a mother and daughter, forcing himself on the daughter and fondling her at knife point while her mother watched. He stole some cash out of their wallets. The two women were terrified, but it was the sort of incident that police didn't take as seriously then as they might today, even though the victims reported it to Allentown police immediately. Krajcir also broke into the house of an elderly woman and groped her. The incident was treated like a case of sexual harassment.

All three women were haunted by the assaults, but at least Krajcir left them alive. Those women would later be haunted by the knowledge that they'd survived an attack by the killer in the blue bandanna, though they never knew why. They would never know what set of circumstances caused them to be the ones who lived.

———————

At some point in the spring of 1983, bolstered by several successful stunts in Pennsylvania—home invasions and sexual assaults—Krajcir was struck again by the urge to kill. One day he sat parked in the lot of a shopping center just to the west of the city of Allentown. The neighborhood was far enough out of the city to not have to worry about a lot of cops around. The shopping center was really more like a strip mall, but the layout may have reminded him of Kroger's in Cape Girardeau.

The lot was sprawling, rimmed by beaten-down row homes on the outskirts of Allentown. The lighting was also poor, making it perfect for Krajcir's needs. As he slouched down in the driver's seat, pistol resting in his lap, loaded and ready to go, he would've spied the woman venturing across the lot to her car, alone.

At this time, another crime spree was in progress in Allentown. Women were being raped. Someone known as the Southside Rapist was preying on women in the Lehigh Valley. Though years later Krajcir would vehemently deny any culpability, he eventually found himself among the suspects. No arrests were ever made in these rape cases, however.

On this particular evening, Krajcir had gone through the exact same motions as he'd done with every one of his previous victims. But the night would end far differently. Something about the car lurking on the edge of the parking lot in the darkness, the form hunched behind the wheel, didn't sit right with the woman. She'd also seen the duct tape wrapped securely over his license plate to conceal the identifying numbers. Common sense told her that no one would do something like that to their car unless they had something to hide. She doubled back to the safety of the store, called the police, and reported "a suspicious person."

Police may have figured it was nothing. Maybe some drunk had passed out in his car. They might not have expected to find the gun. The loaded Excam .25-caliber blue steel pistol lay in Krajcir's lap when the police surprised him. He didn't try to resist; but then he had always been a model prisoner. They also might not have expected to find someone boasting Krajcir's colorful criminal history, with the rape and child molestation and sexual predator offenses glaring at them on his record.

With one phone call from a brave woman, who'd known something about the situation just wasn't right,

Timothy Krajcir's streak of fear and horror came to a screeching halt. He was placed in custody on suspicion of breaking the law against a felon possessing a firearm.

Once Krajcir was in custody for the parole violation, they were able to link him up with the other Allentown crimes. A psychiatrist for the Pennsylvania Department of Probation and Parole evaluated Krajcir in a report that seemed to contradict everything that had ever been written about his mental status until then. This time, Krajcir was described as cold and detached. He told the psychiatrist that the years he'd spent in prison had taught him to stop caring.

Every rape Krajcir had committed was preceded by intense fantasies of sexual abuse and rape, filling his head with hatred before he actually committed the crime. Despite what he'd convinced psychiatrists for years in Illinois, he told this doctor that he'd never really tried to stop himself from raping, and that he didn't particularly care about the consequences of his behavior.

Krajcir felt no remorse for what he did to his victims, though he claimed that he could never hurt someone he knew or with whom he had a personal relationship. He attempted to justify his behavior by linking it to his childhood. He acted out his anger toward his mother on other women, one of the Pennsylvania psychiatrists said. The psychiatrist who said this would only have known about the Pennsylvania mother and daughter Krajcir had assaulted, though by this time Krajcir had also preyed on Grace and Francine, and Mary and Brenda Parsh, and several other women when their children were present.

The more isolated he felt from family and friends, the

worse his behavior got, one of the reasons he cited for the move to Pennsylvania. Perhaps he hoped that living near the area where he'd grown up and spent a large part of his childhood would calm him down, have some sort of placating effect.

A desire to increase his sense of power and control, to compensate for any feelings of inadequacy, drove Krajcir's bitterness toward women. One of the reasons he gave for enjoying his abuse of his former landlord's thirteen-year-old daughter was that he thought her young age meant she'd be more amenable to his needs and requests. She made him feel more masculine.

The psychiatrist recommended a sex offender program that was more intensive than the one he'd been enrolled in previously.

On May 3, 1983, Krajcir attempted to break out of Lehigh County Prison in Allentown. Another inmate cooked up the escape plan with him; both men were in solitary cells on the third tier of the prison. Officials at the prison believed they used a hacksaw to cut a hole in the metal door, and then they fashioned a rope out of bedsheets tied together to lower themselves down the three stories to the ground. The escape didn't exactly work out well for Krajcir: he fell during the descent down the wall and broke his leg. An ambulance had to transport him to a nearby hospital. The other inmate, who faced charges of rape, robbery, theft, aggravated assault, and firearms violations, remained at large.

Shortly after his escape attempt, Krajcir was tried and convicted for the assaults on women he'd committed in Pennsylvania. In addition to the escape attempt, he was found guilty on indecent assault charges, robbery, and criminal trespass. He received a sentence of two and a half to five years in a Pennsylvania prison.

Krajcir served his sentence at the state correctional institution at Graterford. The prison was rough, but again Krajcir became an active participant in his therapy sessions and sex offender program. He convinced officials he was interested in overcoming his urges.

During group therapy sessions, Krajcir repeatedly talked about his strong desire to understand his aggression. He wanted to learn how to resolve his issues with women and work toward a healthy relationship with the fairer sex. He remained a voracious reader, particularly gravitating toward the fields of human sexuality and psychopathology. In therapy, he often played the role of the facilitator, interpreting statements made by the other group members and challenging them to explore their psyches.

Krajcir served out his five-year sentence in Pennsylvania, and then, in 1988, he was sent to Big Muddy Correctional Center in Ina, Illinois, in order to serve out the sentence for his parole violation and violating his conditional release. Since Krajcir was the first person ever committed in Illinois as a sexual predator, the rules were not clear-cut. Perhaps that's why so much had gone wrong when he was evaluated for release.

Krajcir's first mental evaluation when he returned to the psychiatric correctional center in Illinois read like most of the other reports had, years earlier. He was described in a 1988 report as a "coherent, cooperative individual who didn't exhibit any delusions, hallucinations, suicidal or homicidal ideations." The evaluator in that report noted that Krajcir seemed to be well adjusted to his surroundings and was functioning within a bright to normal range of intelligence. Krajcir told psychiatrists that he didn't seek counseling when he was having sexual urges because during those times he was in an extreme amount of emotional stress and was able to rationalize his desires.

At some point after arriving at Big Muddy Correctional Center, however, the man made a decision. Only he knew the terror he'd caused all those women. Only he knew the horror he'd brought to the lives of their families, friends, and communities. Though Krajcir kept so much of what he'd done concealed from authorities, it weighed heavily on his mind.

He decided that he'd never hurt anyone again, and despite all of his reading about the human mind, his quest to understand what fueled his need to hurt women, he could think of only one way to accomplish this. Krajcir stopped his rehabilitation programs cold turkey. It was far too easy, he knew, to convince the therapists that he was healed, that he was committed to his own recovery. They would authorize his conditional release again, and he would rape again, maybe kill again. He did the only thing he could do. He stopped being the perfect patient. Krajcir never attended another therapy session after 1989.

He remained healthy and active in sports while in prison. He was well adjusted within the general population and kept himself occupied. He was never a discipline problem. He had a job at the commissary, where inmates were allowed to purchase phone minutes, food, toiletries, and other essentials. Krajcir had tentatively established a

connection with his brothers and mother again. He felt
that if he went back to group sessions, at some point, his
actions of the last ten years might bubble to the surface of
the discussions. He knew the effect that knowledge of
those crimes would have on his family, and he didn't
want to hurt them. So Krajcir chose to remain silent.
What he'd done would stay a secret for another twenty
years while he lived behind bars.

———————

While Krajcir stayed in prison, investigators from as many
as seven different jurisdictions—the McCracken County
Sheriff's Department in Kentucky, the Carbondale Police
Department in Illinois, the Cape Girardeau Police Department in Missouri, the Paducah Police Department in
Kentucky, the Muhlenberg Township Police Department
in Pennsylvania, the Marion Police Department in Illinois, and the Pennsylvania State Police—continued to
slave over their unsolved murders.

When CODIS, the national DNA database where samples of physical evidence from convicted felons were
stored for testing, was developed for use by federal and
state authorities, detectives in those jurisdictions were
hopeful. At first, the database had a certain magical, be-
all-and-end-all reputation that it couldn't realistically
support. Despite what contemporary forensics television
shows reflect, DNA testing takes months to perform.
Having DNA evidence collected form a crime scene is
not a slam dunk, and it doesn't automatically solve a case.
Police department evidence lockers are full floor to ceiling with boxes containing unknown DNA evidence from

cases that will never be solved. Federal law dictates that this evidence be maintained indefinitely in case new leads crop up, but as time marches on, the likelihood of solving a case drops considerably.

In order to run a DNA sample through CODIS, crime lab technicians need to identify at least thirteen of sixteen core "alleles"—genetic markers—in the unknown sample taken from the crime scene. Those markers are actually spacer DNA, the genetic material found in between the markers that gives us such physical characteristics as blue eyes or blond hair. That spacer DNA is compared one by one to see how many of them in the unknown sample taken from a crime scene can be matched to other profiles from convicted felons contained within the database.

Just because DNA from a crime scene comes back as a "hit" to a felon doesn't mean it automatically solves a case. That DNA sample must then be compared to a fresh sample taken from the felon to obtain a more specific analysis. CODIS is not necessarily meant to solve cases, but to be used as an investigative tool to help narrow down the field of people of interest and home in on a few suspects. Once police zero in on one suspect's DNA, they can easily compare the markers for a more exact match. The accuracy of an identification depends on how many of the sixteen markers that are compared are identical. Without such accuracy, CODIS can only provide a "cannot-exclude" match, meaning that this individual DNA could match that of the unknown sample. With a cannot-exclude result, there's no qualifier for the strength or accuracy of the match.

Samples are taken using a buccal swab, containing genetic material scraped from the inside of the cheek. A sample is then analyzed alongside the evidence from the crime scene for the purpose of matching up as many of the sixteen markers as possible. This sample is usually given voluntarily, but if the individual does not agree to give one, police must get a warrant. To do this, they have to show probable cause for wanting the DNA sample, a requirement that can sometimes throw a wrench in the works if the match is from someone who wouldn't have had access to a crime scene—for example, if they were incarcerated at the time the crime occurred.

The number of markers that lab analysts are able to match, as well as the DNA type, is then entered into a different kind of database designed to create a probability factor to define how many people of the world population are likely to have that exact profile. For example, if four DNA markers of the sixteen are present and match one another, the computer may spit out a statistical match of one in 720,000—meaning that one person among that number of people is likely to have a genetic profile matching that closely to the unknown profile that was tested.

The use of CODIS and DNA testing spurred a new wave of interest in unsolved or "cold" murder cases. Many police departments began assigning these cases full-time to one particular detective so he could work them without any interruption from current investigations. Some larger departments actually formed cold case squads composed of several officers to handle these special homicides.

Unfortunately for the majority of cold case homicides, DNA evidence is not available at every crime scene. Locard's theory of transference, a scientific premise that governs the field of forensics, dictates that no individual can ever interact with another individual without some sort of transfer of elements. Nevertheless, sometimes a killer doesn't leave any DNA behind, no skin cells or strands of hair. At other times, a DNA sample collected at the scene may turn out to contain more than one genetic profile, making it nearly impossible to get an accurate match. Sometimes this happens at the scene, and in other cases it happens when law enforcement passes the sample along to a crime lab through the chain of custody.

So officers must often rely instead on things like tool-mark patterns, soil samples, or fabric fibers. Even if physical material is collected at a crime scene, there's no guarantee it will be a sufficient sample from which to develop a usable genetic profile. Often, crime lab technicians can only develop a partial profile, unsuitable for entry into CODIS.

In 2003, Cape Girardeau found what they hoped was a break in some of their unsolved homicides. Part of the reason they were taking so long to solve could be chalked up to turnover at the police department. As more and more of the investigators who had worked those cases at the time retired or left for work at other agencies, those decades-old murders were no longer at the forefront of the minds of everyone in the detective division. Nevertheless, after years of fruitless struggle with the Margie Call and Mildred Wallace killings, the police finally had a way to link the murders to a suspect.

Detectives submitted blood samples taken from the Call and Wallace crime scenes to the Southeast Missouri

Regional Crime Lab for analysis, the first step toward shedding some light on the twenty-year-old mysteries. The physical evidence in both cases could have been tested earlier. Though only a small amount of blood and semen had been collected from either scene, the ability to multiply it into a testable sample had been around for at least seven years. The technology that allows a crime lab to amplify a minuscule DNA sample taken from a crime scene into something large enough to analyze is called the PCR method. The letters stand for "polymerase chain reaction" and refer to the technique used to replicate cells to make a sample size increase enough so a technician can compare it to another sample. The method mirrors the body's own cell reproduction capabilities, creating the same result in controlled circumstances, so that an identical replication of a tiny amount of genetic material can be accurately reproduced.

Though police generally withhold the names of suspects until they are formally charged by a prosecuting attorney, this time they released a few of the names, including that of Joseph Treanor,[*] a man who'd lived in the same neighborhood as Margie Call and Mildred Wallace. A warrant was obtained for Treanor's DNA in 2003, following a public hearing. Joseph fit the FBI's psychological profile for the women's killer; at the time of the murders, he'd been a twentysomething male, living nearby, and detectives suspected him of having made obscene phone calls from time to time.

---

*Denotes pseudonym

Treanor, using the services of a public defender, had fought the subpoena tooth and nail. He'd battled suspicion of committing these crimes his entire adult life. He'd submitted to having blood drawn back in 1982, and had also been interviewed by investigators at the time. He saw no reason why he should cooperate any further with the investigation, especially twenty years later.

Treanor's blood type didn't match that taken from either crime scene. He felt that this should have been enough to clear him of all suspicion. He also had military papers showing he had been attending boot camp from May to October in 1982 during a brief stint in the U.S. Army. He had been at Fort Leonard Wood on the day that Mildred Wallace was killed. His military career may not have lasted very long, but an alibi from the federal government is about as airtight as it gets.

The original detective on the cases, John Brown, never felt that any of the suspects in either case was strong enough to warrant the high cost of DNA testing. But since the science was there, and it could mean closure for the families of these victims, the department went ahead with it.

Unfortunately, the regional crime lab in Cape Girardeau, blocks from where the murders had occurred, had a backlog of about fifty DNA cases awaiting testing in 2003, so Dr. Robert Briner, the lab's director, made the decision to send the samples to be tested in the state lab. The lab performed about two hundred DNA tests a year in 2003. Murders tended to be rushed straight to the top of the priority list, especially if they were old cases. Nearly a year after the evidence was submitted, the results from the tests performed in the Call and Wallace cases came back.

The DNA test that police had felt certain would finally shed light on the killings turned out to lift all suspicion from the local man, once and for all. When the results were in, the only ones who received closure were Joseph Treanor and two other unnamed suspects. Treanor had lived for years knowing he wasn't a killer. Now his neighbors knew it, too.

As relieved as the man was to have the veil of suspicion finally lifted from his shoulders, he couldn't help feeling frustrated. Police had to have known, between the blood type and his alibi, that he was not the man they were trying to find. Treanor blamed the twenty-year murder investigation for destroying his reputation. He didn't think his relationships would ever recover.

Detective Tracy Lemonds was the head of Cape Girardeau's investigative division, and had been in the department longer than any other detective. He felt the frustration of the entire department when the DNA results came back. They couldn't be entered into CODIS, so there was no hope of finding another suspect, not with the trail of evidence having gone cold years ago. He vowed not to just put the cases back on a shelf and let them gather dust, but he had to be realistic. At this point, he held out little hope that they would ever be solved. The department had just eliminated its top three suspects. Every known rapist and killer living in the area at the time had been flushed out and all of the leads exhausted years ago. Unless the killer appeared out of thin air and

Brenda Parsh (left), and friend Vicki Abernathy, at a Watermelon Queen beauty pageant. Brenda was one of Timothy Krajcir's first murder victims.

—Courtesy of Vicki Abernathy

Southeast Missouri State University student Sheila Cole was shot to death by Timothy Krajcir at a rest stop in McClure, Illinois.

Mildred Wallace, a prominent businesswoman, was murdered by Timothy Krajcir in her Cape Girardeau home in the summer of 1982.

ABOVE:

Cape Girardeau police collect
evidence from the Parsh resi-
dence after the homicides of
Mary and Brenda Parsh.
　　　　—*Courtesy of* Southeast
　　　　　　　　Missourian

RIGHT:

A Cape Girardeau ballistics
examiner test-fires a pistol
into a barrel in an effort to
determine the weapon used in
the Parsh killing.
　　　　—*Courtesy of* Southeast
　　　　　　　　Missourian

ABOVE LEFT:

The rest area in McClure, Illinois, where college student Sheila Cole was found slain. —*Courtesy of the Cape Girardeau County Prosecuting Attorney's Office*

ABOVE RIGHT:

Sheila Cole's Chevy Nova was found abandoned at the Cape Girardeau Wal-Mart before her body was discovered across the Mississippi River in Illinois.
—*Courtesy of the Cape Girardeau County Prosecuting Attorney's Office*

Police gather evidence and prepare to take crime scene photos in front of the home of Mildred Wallace. —*Courtesy of* Southeast Missourian

The broken window of the Margie Call residence, which Krajcir
used to enter the home.
—*Courtesy of the Cape Girardeau County Prosecuting Attorney's Office*

ABOVE LEFT:

Krajcir typically gained entrance to his victims' homes by breaking a
bathroom window.
—*Courtesy of the Cape Girardeau County Prosecuting Attorney's Office*

ABOVE RIGHT:

The shattered bathroom window of the Parsh residence.
—*Courtesy of the Cape Girardeau County Prosecuting Attorney's Office*

Margie Call's bathroom, with broken glass visible on the rug.

—Courtesy of the Cape Girardeau County Prosecuting Attorney's Office

Toiletries fell from Mildred Wallace's bathroom windowsill at some point during the break-in.

—Courtesy of the Cape Girardeau County Prosecuting Attorney's Office

Krajcir waited inside the Parsh residence and grabbed Mary and Brenda Parsh as they returned home from the airport.

—Courtesy of the Cape Girardeau County Prosecuting Attorney's Office

ABOVE:

Krajcir also lay in wait for Mildred Wallace, attacking her as she came home from visiting a family member.

—Courtesy of the Cape Girardeau County Prosecuting Attorney's Office

RIGHT:

Krajcir cut the cord on the telephone of Mildred Wallace's kitchen while he waited for her to return.

—Courtesy of the Cape Girardeau County Prosecuting Attorney's Office

LEFT:

Bullet fragment recovered from the home of Mildred Wallace.

—*Courtesy of the Cape Girardeau County Prosecuting Attorney's Office*

BELOW:

Top mug: Timothy Krajcir, 1988, within the Illinois Department of Corrections after returning to Illinois on a parole violation to serve the remainder of his sentence. Bottom mug: Krajcir received parole from the state of Illinois and was released from Menard Psychiatric Center in 1981.

—*Courtesy of the Illinois Department of Corrections*

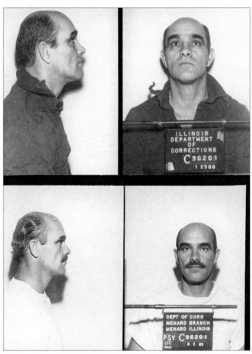

Krajcir in court in Jackson County, Illinois, to plead guilty to murder of Deborah Sheppard.
—*Aaron Eisenhauer*/Southeast Missourian

Timothy Krajcir, escorted to court by corrections officers in Jackson County, Illinois for a plea hearing in the Deborah Sheppard killing.
—*Aaron Eisenhauer*/Southeast Missourian

Krajcir appears in a Cape Girardeau, Missouri, courtroom to face five murder charges.
—*Fred Lynch*/Southeast Missourian

confessed to the murders, Lemonds didn't see how he would ever mark the cases "closed."

In May of 2007, responsibility for all of Cape Girardeau's unsolved homicides, including the killings of Mary and Brenda Parsh, Sheila Cole, Margie Call, and Mildred Wallace, were transferred to Detective Jimmy Smith, who became the department's first cold case detective.

Chapter 8

Unraveling a Cold Case

Detective Lieutenant Paul Echols lived in Carbondale during the same time as Timothy Krajcir; in fact, his house was on the same street as the trailer that the killer had rented. Their paths very possibly crossed, either on Springer Street, or at Southern Illinois University, where they both worked toward the same degree in criminal justice administration at the same time.

While at SIU, Echols met Carl Kinnison, who would later work on the Margie Call homicide and become the Cape Girardeau chief of police. The two men became friends, and kept in touch after graduation.

Echols has boyish looks, a dark blond mop of hair with a touch of gray, an open face, and eyes with a friendly twinkle. While Detective Jimmy Smith usually favors dark suits, tailored white shirts, and crimson ties, regardless of the occasion, Echols dresses in a more relaxed fashion, and he keeps in shape by running on his lunch breaks at the Carbondale Police Department. Until the Krajcir case, Smith and Echols had never met.

Carbondale chief of police Bob Ledbetter handed the Deborah Sheppard cold case files over to Echols in 2006. Echols had already proven his skill at cold case investigation when he'd solved the murder of Susan Schumacke, a young, attractive brunette, not unlike Brenda Parsh, who had been raped and killed one night along one of the footpaths at Southern Illinois University. Suspicion for the murder had fallen on John Phillips, a known killer who'd been living in the area at the time, but Echols wasn't convinced he was their man. Phillips was deceased by 2006, so Echols pursued a warrant to exhume the man's body, and was able to use DNA evidence to prove that the killer was not Phillips but another man, Daniel Woloson. Woloson was tried and convicted of the homicide.

After the Schumacke case was closed, Ledbetter wanted Echols to work on the Sheppard homicide. He delved into the twenty-year-old mystery the same way he'd approached the Schumacke case, via forensics. After twenty years of dead ends, a CODIS hit returned a solid lead: Timothy Wayne Krajcir.

Krajcir's DNA sample would have been added to CODIS sometime in the early to mid 1990s, when crime lab analysts across the nation became obsessed with the genetic material. Because he was a convicted felon and had been since CODIS was implemented, his sample would have been added as a matter of protocol.

At the time, all that the detective knew about Krajcir

was that he'd spent the last twenty-four years of his life in prison. Echols learned about the 1979 child molestation case, and about the 1963 rape in Illinois. Moreover, he realized that Krajcir must have voluntarily kept himself in prison, because there were all sorts of programs of which he could have taken advantage to gain early release. The civil commitment wasn't designed to be a life sentence, merely a way for the state to keep track of some of its most dangerous sexual predators.

Echols obtained a DNA sample from Krajcir—a fresh buccal swab—for comparison purposes. The DNA analysis of the Sheppard samples came back a 1 out of 1.98 quadrillion, meaning that only one individual out of that number of people—more people than are on the entire planet—was likely to have that particular genetic profile. Echols interviewed Krajcir about Deborah Sheppard on a multitude of occasions. Each time, Krajcir denied ever having being in her apartment, meeting her, or killing her. When he was confronted with the DNA results, however, there was little he could say by way of denial.

Eventually, Echols forged enough of a rapport with Krajcir to persuade him to confess in detail to the murder of Deborah Sheppard. He spent hours talking to Krajcir, getting to know him as a person, not only as a suspect. In spite of himself, Echols found himself liking the other man. He had also become close to Bernard Sheppard, the victim's father, and he was determined to bring the family closure after so many years of heartbreaking frustration.

Finally, Krajcir agreed to plead guilty. He would not be subjected to the death penalty, but he could potentially receive a life sentence, or forty years, a guarantee that he'd never see the light of freedom again, given his age.

The Sheppards expressed gratitude to Krajcir for coming clean in the end. He'd answered questions that had haunted them for two decades. He'd given the parents of the bright, pretty twenty-three-year-old the closure they'd craved for years.

Krajcir's arrest for the twenty-five-year-old homicide was national news. A photo of the bespectacled Timothy Krajcir appeared in newspapers all over Missouri and Illinois. The *Chicago Tribune* put it on the front page. Jimmy Smith happened to catch the Channel Twelve news the morning the arrest story ran. He was eating breakfast when he saw the segment about Deborah Sheppard, and the quest to find her killer. There on the screen was a Carbondale detective, talking about how he'd solved the case, put together the fractured pieces of a murder mystery most had all but given up on.

The name Timothy Krajcir didn't ring a bell with Smith, who had been appointed to investigate cold cases for Cape Girardeau in March of 2007. Surely, he thought, he would have recognized a name that unusual. Years ago, the detectives who worked those cases—Brown and Ray Johnson—had flushed out the name of every single criminal living within a hundred miles who was likely to prey on women. This man's name, Smith thought, would surely have cropped up during previous investigations. Like everyone else, Smith wasn't certain how to pronounce the man's name, and he certainly didn't think Krajcir had any ties to Cape Girardeau. But he had to admit that his curiosity had been piqued, especially since

Carbondale was less than an hour away from Cape Girardeau.

Assigning a full-time detective to the department's unsolved homicides had been a gutsy move on Chief Kinnison's part. Cape Girardeau had never been able to devote such resources to its cold cases. For years, five photographs, some of them in black and white, had hung on the bulletin board in the Cape Girardeau Police Department: those of Mary Parsh, the doting mother, and her adoring daughter Brenda hung side by side, the same way they'd been killed. The smile in Sheila Cole's photograph was shy and timid, suggesting that she'd been too fearful in the end to fight off her attacker. Margie Call's picture epitomized the kindly, cheerful grandmother her loved ones remembered. Mildred Wallace seemed stern in her picture, her smile businesslike.

Five lives snuffed out too early, five faces adorning a wall every officer had to pass by each day, reminding them to keep an eye out for their killer as they patrolled the streets of Cape Girardeau that day.

Over the years, nearly every detective had taken a turn reading through the cases, hoping for fresh insights, but turning the investigations over to Smith sent a message that Kinnison, one of the first responders on two of the homicides, and the Cape Girardeau Police Department had every intention of closing these cases and bringing some long-awaited closure to the victims' families.

Detective Smith called Detective Lieutenant Echols and introduced himself. Echols was sympathetic, and interested in hearing about the long-unsolved cases, but he didn't believe he could help Smith. In all of the interviews

Echols had conducted with Krajcir, the man never once mentioned Cape Girardeau. Echols, of course, knew the nearby town well. He'd taken his wife on many a date there before they'd been married. His sister lived and worked in Cape Girardeau. Still, he'd come across no information during the course of the Sheppard investigation that would've led him to think Krajcir had ever set foot in the town.

Based on Sheppard's murder, and Krajcir's subsequent confession to the crime, Echols had assembled a profile of a typical Krajcir murder. He presented the profile to Smith, and then began contacting law enforcement jurisdictions all over the state of Illinois, putting feelers out for any unsolved homicides that might resemble this profile.

At first, this tactic seemed to be another dead end. Deborah Sheppard had not been killed in the same manner as any of the Cape Girardeau victims—no broken bathroom window, no bound hands. But then, as Smith prepared to return to unraveling the endless tangle of potential suspects in the cases, something caught his attention. He'd been going through every unsolved homicide and rape case in Cape Girardeau that coincided with Krajcir's years of activity when he found one that looked like a match to Krajcir's pattern: in 1982, a woman named Leslie Marcano had been raped, and police never arrested anyone for the crime. The victim had given a clear and poignant description of what had happened to her during the sexual assault. It seemed to Smith as if every detail correlated with the profile that Echols had created.

Suddenly there seemed to be a distinct possibility that Krajcir had been Leslie's rapist.

Smith hesitantly called Leslie. He didn't want to give her any false hope that her assailant had been found, but it was important that he talk with her and make certain that the details they had were correct. The account she gave was exactly the same as it had been earlier, and after seeing a picture of Krajcir circa 1983, she said she believed he was the man who'd assaulted her.

Now police had a way of placing Krajcir in Cape Girardeau in 1982. It was a stronger lead than any they'd gotten in a long, long while, but it didn't necessarily make him a killer.

Detectives Jimmy Smith and Tracy Lemonds, the supervisor of the detective division, began reviewing all of the physical evidence in the cases. They submitted semen samples from the Mildred Wallace case for comparison with samples from Krajcir, and they quietly began learning more about their new suspect while they waited for the results. The DNA test returned a statistical match of 1 in 720,000. Smith thought this was promising, but Lemonds remained unconvinced. The match wasn't particularly strong.

Along with the physical evidence taken from the crime scene, they had submitted the partial palm print the killer had left behind as he leaned against the window, waiting for the older woman to return home. David Warren had been the crime lab technician who'd collected the evidence at some of those crime scenes decades earlier. He and Lemonds had worked together on gathering the evidence from Margie Call's house. When Warren realized how closely Timothy Krajcir's palm prints matched the one they'd found at Wallace's house, he picked up the phone and called Lemonds.

The discovery rocked the entire police department. Every officer had seen the faces of those women. Every one of them was aware of the ramifications of what had just occurred: they'd unraveled Cape Girardeau's most vexing mystery, and the biggest threat to the safety and peace of mind of its residents.

It seemed like a sound assumption that if Krajcir had raped Leslie Marcano and killed Mildred Wallace in 1982, he'd also killed Margie Call. But they still had no way of knowing whether Krajcir had killed the other three women in 1977, or if he'd even been in the area during that time. Then an inmate who'd been in the same prison as Krajcir mentioned to a guard that he'd heard Krajcir bragging about raping the same women twice in Cape Girardeau.

Leslie was still so traumatized by what she'd suffered all those years ago that it was difficult for her to accept phone calls from the Cape Girardeau Police Department. Knowing the identity of her attacker, having to look at his picture, see his face, and confirm the horrors he'd committed against her had taken a big emotional toll. She'd formed something of a bond with Chief Kinnison, who tried not to call her often because he knew how upsetting his calls were. But a few weeks after she made the identification of her attacker and Krajcir, her phone rang again, again it was the police department, and at last she was asked the question she'd so long been dreading. There was no kind or tactful way to pose it: Had she also been raped in 1977? The answer, of course, was yes, followed by heart-wrenching sobs.

Now detectives could positively link Timothy Krajcir to Cape Girardeau during both waves of murders. He had prowled the streets of Cape Girardeau in 1977. The time frames matched up perfectly. The attack on Leslie in the parking lot of the Wal-Mart had occurred a few months before the slaying of the Parsh women. Reason told them if he'd committed both of those crimes in Cape Girardeau, the chances were strong that he'd committed others as well. Maybe he'd even committed crimes that had never been reported.

They had physical evidence incriminating Krajcir in the killing of Mildred Wallace, and they had circumstantial evidence that he'd committed some of the other murders. Now they only had to get some answers from him.

Chapter 9

Confessions

NOVEMBER 14, 2007

Carbondale, Illinois, detective lieutenant Paul Echols spoke quickly, as though he were nervous. Years and years of investigative work were riding on this interview. At 10 A.M., Echols sat waiting for the arrival of Timothy Krajcir in an interview room at Big Muddy Correctional Center in Ina, Illinois.

Beside him sat Cape Girardeau, Missouri, detective Jimmy Smith. They'd agreed it would just be the two of them today. This was the icebreaking interview, the one that would hopefully set the stage to convince Krajcir to confess. They were aiming for as open and detailed a confession as Echols had gotten from him in the Sheppard killing. They wanted details; they *needed* the details that had deliberately been kept out of the press for decades so they'd have a way of gauging whether or not he told the truth.

The interview room was tiny, lined with eggshell-colored brick. A low table and black-backed chairs were the only furnishings. There was an odd echo.

Krajcir shuffled into the room, his drab brown garb enveloping his slouched frame and giving him a hunchbacked appearance. The department-issued uniform resembled a monk's robe. Krajcir's arms were chalk white, deprived of sunlight for the last twenty-five years. Faded ink from several tattoos, including one of a rose, stood out against the ghostly skin.

Echols spoke first.

"Hey, Tim," he began hesitantly.

"Hi," the inmate replied softly.

"How are you?" Echols asked.

"All right." Krajcir gave a hushed response.

Echols offered him a cup of fresh coffee, and the older man politely accepted. He took it black.

Echols explained that he would need to read Krajcir his Miranda rights, just as they had done before. They had been slowly getting into a routine with each other during these interviews. Echols knew that Krajcir had heard Miranda so many times by now he could probably recite it back to the detectives. He told him he had the right to stay quiet and not incriminate himself. He had the right to have an attorney present, and that one would need to be appointed by the court, since Krajcir had no source of income. Krajcir signed a waiver acknowledging that he understood the rights that had just been explained to him. They were ready to get down to business.

"I'm not here to ask you any questions about the Deborah Sheppard case," Echols said.

Then he realized that Krajcir would probably be interested in knowing how the Sheppard family felt about his confession. Echols was beginning to realize that the perception others held of him was very important to Krajcir.

Echols had finally gotten a chance to meet the family face-to-face, and they'd had a conversation about Timothy Krajcir.

"They told me privately that, ah, I mean while they're obviously not happy with what happened, they do appreciate the fact that you did come forward. It has allowed their family to have a lot of closure," he said.

The interview began with small talk. Krajcir spoke about his trip to Carbondale the day before for a hearing. Nothing happened at the hearing, and he seemed to think the trip had been a waste.

He said he'd enjoyed the ride, though.

Krajcir was still in segregation, he told Echols and Smith when they asked him what had been going on. He'd been placed in segregation ever since the charges had been filed for the murder of Deborah Sheppard. Echols speculated that the move may have been designed to keep him safe in case some of the black inmates took issue with the fact that Krajcir had murdered a black woman. Krajcir wasn't happy with the situation, and didn't like the segregation at all.

Echols finally got around to telling Krajcir why they were there. If Krajcir was surprised by their intentions, he didn't show it.

"There are a couple of old cases that we've looked into, and we believe it's you," Echols said.

He wanted to bring closure to the families of victims in those cases, too, he explained. Authorities had been doing a lot of forensic testing, Echols told him. A lot of the tests were still pending, no physical evidence had ever been collected in some of the cases, and the evidence in others was too far deteriorated to be of any use to a lab.

The first of the old cases Echols described for Krajcir concerned sexual assaults. He mentioned a Johnston City, Illinois, and two Marion, Illinois, assaults. One of them had occurred in March of 1982, and involved an older woman who lived alone. The perpetrator entered her house through a window, brandished a gun, and ambushed her when she returned from church. His face had been hidden by a piece of fabric. He tied her hands before sexually assaulting her.

"This lady is still alive. There are two or three out there that are still alive," Echols said.

The victim in the 1982 assault had immediately moved out of her home because she couldn't bring herself to stay there after what had happened. Echols had just spoken with one of her friends the day before, and he knew that the assault still weighed very heavily on her mind.

"I would like to be able to tell her that the person who did this has some remorse. He's sorry for it and just bring an end to that," Echols told Krajcir.

Krajcir nodded slowly, appearing to listen, but then said no, he couldn't do that in this case.

"I very seldom went over to Marion," Krajcir said.

Echols moved on to describe the rape committed in

Johnston City. In that case, an older couple had been at home when the offender surprised them. He got in through the back door. He tied the man up on the floor, bound the woman's hands, and led her into a bedroom, where he proceeded to assault her.

"I'm here shooting straight with you. I've treated you good," Echols said.

The man who'd been a victim of that assault was dead, but his wife was still alive. She probably had only a few years left. She was in her nineties. Echols wanted to be able to give her the peace of mind that could only come with knowing her attacker was safely behind bars, and that he wouldn't be creeping through her back door again. She deserved to know he'd been caught, and that she was safe.

The third case also happened in Marion, Illinois. The woman had been in her late eighties. An armed suspect got into her and her husband's house while they were relaxing on the back porch. When they went inside, the perpetrator tied their hands and assaulted the woman. This assault was nearly identical to the Johnston City case. None of the evidence in these cases had been tested, but Echols warned Krajcir that he might have to authorize those tests if he didn't get cooperation.

Echols referenced another sexual assault, one that occurred on North Almond Street in Carbondale. The police had spoken with Krajcir about the assault shortly after it occurred. He had lived on Springer Street, which ran parallel to Almond. Although Krajcir had successfully avoided detection back then, he was known as a sex offender, and the proximity of his residence to the scene of a rape made it impossible for him to slip under the radar.

"That's when they had that big snowstorm," Krajcir recalled.

He remembered he'd been living for a couple months at the Carbondale Mobile Home Park when eighteen inches of snow fell on the city in just one day.

Echols also remembered the snowstorm, because they'd shut the interstate down. At the time he was working at a gas station to help pay his college tuition. It was the heaviest snowfall he could ever recall experiencing.

Frustrated with what seemed to him to be a lack of focus on Krajcir's part, Echols tried again to persuade him to come clean.

"The reason I come to you to talk is [that you're] not the same Tim that was having these issues back in those days. I know you talked about the fact that this was something you couldn't control. But the fact [is] that you've controlled it by staying in prison and not going to the counseling, and by that you've essentially sentenced yourself to stay in jail the rest of your life. In prison the rest of your life. I don't know that that will ever change, but trying to get to the bottom of these situations and get the truth from you . . . I think it also opens you up to be able to start your programming again at some point. If you choose to do so. Now, you had told me before that one of the reasons you couldn't go to the program was because you couldn't open up and be honest with everybody," Echols said.

He paused to allow his words to sink in, to register with the man sitting in front of him. Krajcir had already moved partway toward his recovery by choosing to remain behind bars, Echols pointed out. At some point, it might behoove him to return to the sex offender programs and get some help. No one would ever be able to respect the man Krajcir had been when he'd killed Deborah Sheppard. The choices he'd made since then, however, were more acceptable, decent, even admirable, Echols told him.

"If you had stayed out and about, I'm afraid you're right. You probably couldn't have controlled it," Echols said.

The fact that Krajcir recognized this about himself, knew that more people could get hurt if he was on the outside, and had done the only thing he could to control his urges had been an admirable decision on his part.

Krajcir acted as though he really wished he could help, but he knew nothing about the assaults that Echols had just described. He'd only been to Marion a couple of times, once to transport a patient to the hospital there when he'd been an EMT. Another time he'd made plans to visit Marion, during the tornado of 1982, but his then girl-friend had called him at the last minute and he'd changed his mind.

Echols again reiterated that he was only trying to bring some comfort to the women who'd been the victims of those crimes.

"When these women suffer through these events like that, they never forget it. They look over their shoulder for the rest of their lives," he said. He wanted to spare them from having to deal with this for the rest of their lived.

The interview became a stalemate—until Detective Jimmy Smith began to pepper Krajcir with questions.

"Tim, did you say it wasn't you in those cases? Do you

remember anything about those cases? See any news at that time?" he asked.

Krajcir didn't answer right away. He stuttered, obviously unprepared for the questions.

"Read anything about it? Hear anything about it?" Smith pressed on.

"I didn't hear anything," Krajcir replied quietly.

He went on to say that he'd rarely gotten to watch the news because he'd worked the night shift back then. He usually only used his television to watch sports.

"I don't know whether I told you or not," Echols said to Smith, "but Tim was apparently a very good athlete earlier and actually not too long ago, is what I understand. I've had at least one gentleman call me from DOC [the department of corrections], which worked with Tim when he was at Menard, and told me he was the best basketball player he'd ever seen."

Krajcir said he'd only recently quit playing sports in prison, and had begun to officiate them.

"Basketball was my favorite sport," Smith said "I've played a lot of basketball. I'm sixty-one and you said you're sixty-two."

Krajcir was actually sixty-three at this time, but they were still nearly the same age, Smith pointed out.

"Unlike you and I, he's kept his hair," Echols joked to Krajcir.

Moving on from the sports talk, Echols voiced the reason why he'd brought Smith along on this interview.

"Jim is here with the Cape Girardeau Police Department. Cape Girardeau has some cases on you," he said. "I'm not gonna make any bones about it."

He went on to explain that the department had already done some of the forensics work on their unsolved cases. They also had a positive identification from a photo lineup.

"It was a black lady and her daughter. Nice-looking black lady," Smith said, referring to Leslie Marcano. "She lived on the west side of town. Do you remember where the fairgrounds was located?"

Krajcir made negative sounds and shook his head no.

"She lived in a new building out there and she was preparing to mop her floor one night and she was going to throw some water out the back door in a bucket," Smith continued. When the woman opened the door, someone stuck their foot in the door and forced their way in, a gun in hand. The intruder forced mother and daughter to lie on the floor, and sexually assaulted the mother. The date was January 9, 1982.

Then Smith dropped the bomb: "So she's also picked you out of a photo lineup," he said smoothly.

Smith mentioned that Leslie was religious, something he hoped would jog Krajcir's memory.

Echols again pointed out that knowing the truth behind her attack might give this woman closure.

"I know the Tim [who] was involved with these cases is totally different from the guy I've kind of gotten to know in the interviews. So I guess the question is, does the Tim today [take] responsibility for acknowledging . . . the evil part of what you did back in those days?" Echols wondered aloud.

Smith thought he could help with this one. He and Leslie Marcano had actually worked together at one point back in the eighties. He had had no idea of the extent of her suffering, that she had been violated not once but twice, but he recognized her demeanor, the averted eyes and soft manner of speech, and felt her trauma.

"I know this lady personally and I used to work with her many years ago . . . She has a hard time discussing any of what happened to her and her daughter," Smith said. He described how Leslie's daughter had refused to return to Cape Girardeau, not even for a visit. Smith also thought it was time the two women gained some hard-won comfort in their lives. He, too, appreciated the fact that Krajcir knew he was dangerous, and had deliberately kept himself incarcerated all those years. As a cop, Smith was grateful for this.

Echols again brought up the Sheppard family, and the closure that Krajcir's confession had brought to them. He'd like other families who'd lost loved ones to be able to have that kind of closure.

"Been involved in the investigation of this case quite a bit, and there's no doubt in my mind that it's you," Echols told him.

"Well, there's no doubt in her mind, it is Tim," Smith added quickly.

Krajcir refused to admit to the assault.

"Uh-uh, didn't do it." He shook his head firmly.

"Did you ever go to Cape?" Echols wanted to know.

"Occasionally. My girl's best friend went to school down there," Krajcir replied.

"Who did? I'm sorry," Echols said.

"A girl I was going with at the time," he elaborated. His chest still bore a rose tattoo emblazoned with her name, Marlene. "Her best friend went to school down there. And once a month, we'd drive her down there."

Suddenly the interview had taken a turn toward intensity. The questions came rapid-fire, and Krajcir's answers were clipped.

"She was from Carbondale."

"Yeah."

"Did you have any friends in Cape during those years?" Smith asked.

"No."

"Did you know anyone at all?"

"No."

"Did Marlene work for the ambulance service or the hospital?"

"No . . . Carbondale Memorial Hospital."

Later in the interview, Smith and Echols circled back to this subject. Echols explained that he'd taken it upon himself to find out everything he could about Timothy Krajcir. He'd talked to everyone he could find who had known Krajcir when he was younger. He'd looked at a lot of cases from years ago. He called what he'd found a "debris field." He considered it his job to try to clean up this field.

"And that's why I'm here. Obviously you did spend some time around Cape Girardeau," Echols said.

"Did you frequent any bars or businesses in Cape Girardeau during those years?" Smith asked.

"I never went down there that much other than when we took Nancy [Marlene's friend] down there," Krajcir insisted.

"Mm-hmm." Smith still sounded wholly unconvinced.

191

Krajcir added that he'd been to Cape Girardeau several times with the ambulance service, to one of the two hospitals.

Echols returned to Nancy, Marlene's friend and a former coworker of Krajcir's, whom the detective had recently spoken to.

"She's a nice gal," Krajcir said, remembering.

"She sure had a lot of good things to say about you . . . I mean . . . like everybody I've talked to, [she was] pretty amazed that you were involved in some of the things that you were. It's like there's two Tims. And I keep seeing that," Echols said.

"Yeah, I agree to that," Krajcir said.

"Was there two Tims? Is that . . ."

"Pretty much," Krajcir nodded.

"And I guess like you said, when you get one of these impulses to go out and do something, that was the other Tim," Echols guessed.

"Yeah, rationality went out the window," Krajcir said.

Smith asked him about alcohol. Krajcir said he wasn't a heavy drinker, and he'd never used drugs, not really.

"I've been twisted since I was a little kid. Can't blame it on nothing else. The first six or seven years of my life I was left alone too much. And it twisted me," he said.

Smith made a sympathetic sound of comprehension, but didn't say anything.

"It just got worse when I grew up, I guess," Krajcir said.

Krajcir explained that he had two half brothers. One brother joined the army, and actually turned out pretty good, in Krajcir's opinion.

"You know you said you've been twisted for a long time and you thought it had happened when you were a young child. About being left alone. Were you sexually abused? Physically abused?" Smith asked.

"No . . . no, it was all emotional," Krajcir answered.

Krajcir said he'd been left to his own devices frequently from the time he was a year old till he was about six. When he was four, he'd pushed his younger brother off their front porch and broken his leg.

At five, he broke into a neighbor's house and trashed the place. At eight, he was placed on probation for stealing a bicycle.

When he was fourteen, he took to burglarizing and indulging in acts of voyeurism at nearly every opportunity that presented itself.

"I had no father. And my mother was never there. And . . . and a child that young, you have to have something from a female or . . . a father . . ." Krajcir's voice trailed off softly.

"I agree," Smith said.

"Some kind of, you know . . . attention. If you don't you just go twisted." Krajcir knew he'd gone twisted.

It sounded as though he'd gotten a much better grip on his past now, Smith said. He probably wouldn't ever know the exact reasons for his behavior, but at least he understood some of the way his early years had formed his personality.

"Probably. Probably. Unless I just . . . somehow getting back at a mom that was never there or something, I . . . don't know," Krajcir said.

"You know," Echols mused, "you're probably the

smartest guy I've ever talked with or interviewed on these sides of the walls, and it is interesting to talk to you . . . One of the big things that's interesting is the fact that you seem to have figured out yourself . . . I mean, I know you've been through a lot of psychological testing and interviews and you've talked with psychiatrists and tried to figure out what's going on, but the interesting fact is . . . I don't know if they ever figured it out, but it seems like you have pretty much self-diagnosed yourself."

"Yeah, that's fair," Krajcir agreed.

"And it obviously keeps coming back to the fact that in that self-diagnosis you have been able to remove yourself from society. I don't know anybody that . . . that's ever been . . . able to do that," Echols added.

Experience told him that most disturbed people deny that they have a problem, and keep on behaving the same way, even if it lands them behind bars. Then they work on getting out, serving their time, and then repeat the same behaviors that got them into trouble before.

He'd seen it happen, Krajcir said.

"I guess that gave you incentive to realize that . . . I think you even said this, that if you went back out . . . there would be a chance that you might hurt somebody again," Echols pointed out.

"No, I *knew*," Krajcir corrected.

"That reflects so much, but what do we do with the old stuff? What do we do with the things that happened when you were out? I mean, do we just leave them alone and let them linger until the people die? Or do we try to make something good out of something that was so bad? . . . What can you reap out of all this . . . ?" An imploring note seemed to creep into Echols's voice at this point. He asked Krajcir again about Leslie.

"Wasn't me," Krajcir repeated, but he hesitated for a split second before shaking his head.

Echols had to know. "This Tim or the other Tim?"

"This Tim," Krajcir said.

"There are kind of two of them here, so . . . were there times that you just don't remember what you did?" Echols asked.

"No. I told you most of the stuff that I did. I mean there's a lot of little incident things that I did, you know . . . like all of that exposure that I did . . ." Krajcir said.

He had told them most of everything he'd done; he said he described it already.

At this juncture, Smith spoke up for the first time in several minutes.

"I know we're talking to at least two Tims and it's a little bit difficult for me to understand that sometimes . . . I'm not gonna sit here and try to pretend I know what makes you tick. This is my first time to ever talk with you . . . and it's hard for me to understand this. You know, you say that there was another person and it's somebody from years ago. And I appreciate that. But in forgiving yourself for what you may or may not have done years ago—"

"Well, I have never done that," Krajcir said quietly.

Smith suggested that maybe Krajcir could find forgiveness in giving people like Leslie and her daughter the opportunity to know who he was.

"You know that can be done," Smith said.

"Does it matter that I said that Mrs. Sheppard forgave

you? Does that mean anything to you at all?" Echols sounded frustrated.

"Ah . . . it's nice, but . . ." Krajcir's answer was noncommittal.

"Yeah. Well, it's huge on the other end," Echols said.

"Yeah," Krajcir said.

"It really is. It's huge. Because not only does that resonate through us, in law enforcement, but it also [resonates] with the rest of her family. It's an event. It's a tragic event that will carry through the generations. The same way with this. I mean, the situation with . . . the rape that took place, you know, the little girl [Leslie's daughter] was eleven years old. And thankfully you didn't rape her. And . . . and you know it's hard to commend in such an event, but the fact that you didn't do that, that's great. Or the little girl would have been even more traumatized. The fact that she can't even come back to the town to see her mother because of the event . . . if she just knew you were here and had taken responsibility for that . . . then maybe that would change their lives," Echols said.

"You can't be locked up any more than forever, you know. Forever's forever," Smith pointed out.

Krajcir insisted, "I can't do it. It wasn't me. Someone that might have resembled me maybe, but it wasn't me."

Echols asked him about the prison counseling sessions. He wanted to know if he had talked about things like this during these times.

"Is that where you actually [did] discuss some of the things that occurred in the past?" he asked.

"Yes."

"So that's why you have to be honest to actually go into those," Echols said.

"If you're not honest, there ain't no sense in going. And then [you're] just . . . fooling yourself," Krajcir replied.

He thought he would eventually start going to the sessions again.

"Okay, well, I don't think you're going to be able to until you come clean in this one," Echols told him.

Echols was having a hard time understanding Krajcir's reluctance to admit to the rape. The man was already in prison. Law enforcement had nothing to gain except the closure they wanted to bring to the families. They weren't trying to make sure Krajcir stayed in prison, because at this point, he was never going to get out.

"Now, you know one of the things that you told me is talking about all the lies that . . . you told through years to protect yourself, and of course you did that with the Sheppard case as well. And then you had told me that it was time to quit lying. And . . . I still don't feel like you're coming . . . well, I know you're not being truthful with me now," Echols said.

Smith wanted to know how Krajcir had reached his decision to confess to Echols about killing Deborah Sheppard.

"I think a lot of it, I just wanted to get it off my mind, I think. I'd . . . I'd figured at one time or another some of this was going to catch up with me," Krajcir admitted.

He'd said before that he planned on coming clean in a

few years when his health started to fail. He would give full disclosure on everything then.

Krajcir didn't consider himself to be an overly religious person. He did believe in God, though, and knew at some point he'd have to stand before Him and be judged. That was going to be a tough one, he knew that. He didn't know if the two men sitting across the table believed that to be true, but he did. He also believed that if he asked for forgiveness, and if the forgiveness he was granted came from the heart, his burden would be lifted.

"You know, I've done some things in my life that I haven't been real pleased with either. We all make mistakes. We all do. We're all sinners. But we can also ask for forgiveness," Smith told him.

Smith brought up the example of Mrs. Sheppard. She'd been able to forgive Krajcir.

"And I don't know if you get any comfort out of that, but you probably should. What do you feel about that?" Smith asked.

"Well, I'm not real religious so . . ." Krajcir began.

He was glad that Deborah's mother had forgiven him, but it didn't seem to affect him much deeper than that.

"Well, you know it's commendable that you wanted to wait till you got older, but in a way, that's kind of selfish, too, because you're doing it on your own terms . . . once again not thinking about the victims. Because some of these victims, well, one of the ladies in Marion is not even alive anymore. As you wait for your right time to do it, once again, not having any consideration for anybody else either. Does that make sense?" Echols said.

Krajcir murmured another noncommittal reply.

"So you're saying it wasn't you and you're not gonna change that," Echols said.

"No," Krajcir said.

"You are a smart enough man . . . I am not going to sit here and badger you. I am not going to do that. I have more respect for you than that," Echols said.

He said he wouldn't ask Krajcir anything more about the unsolved rapes. He did, however, ask him to give the matter a lot of thought. Echols knew in his heart and mind that he'd found the perpetrator of those crimes. He knew he wasn't wrong.

"And I swear to you that it is my goal to take back to these old ladies before they die the fact that the person who did this thing to them years ago has accepted responsibility and says hey, you know the last year or two of your life, don't be afraid, don't be looking over your shoulder. He is sorry for what he did," Echols said.

He wanted to be able to go back and tell Krajcir's victims that the man who had violated them was incarcerated, and part of the reason was because he accepted responsibility within his own heart.

Detective Smith wasn't quite ready to throw in the towel that day, however. He returned to the sexual assaults against Leslie, and described the first of them.

"She left Wal-Mart in Cape Girardeau with her daughter, who was five years old at the time, they were approaching their car. Forced into the vehicle. She was made to lie on the person's lap. The little girl was in the back, covered up and told to be quiet or she would be hurt. She was driven probably across the Mississippi Bridge, mostly, she thinks, and during that time she was forced to commit sexual acts on the person. She says it's you," Smith informed Krajcir.

"She said both times it was you. And we believe her," Echols added.

He asked if they needed to come back with some evidence.

"No, wasn't me," Krajcir said.

The DNA technology was catching up with him, Echols told him.

"We're not going to sit here and tell you everything," Smith added, "and in turn get nothing from you. Do you believe in DNA? What do you know about DNA?"

Krajcir quietly answered that he knew a little.

"I think Paul hit the nail on the head, that you're not gonna talk about anything unless we got something, scientifically, to lay in front of you, right. We can get that cleared up right now, I assume," Smith guessed.

"Well, I've . . . I've talked about everything I've done. And a . . . I think I'm just gonna stop . . . stop talking, period," Krajcir said.

Echols informed him that Cape Girardeau did have DNA evidence in one of their cases. Smith was going to tell him about that one.

Slowly, methodically, Smith described the murder of Mildred Wallace.

"Lived alone. Never been married. She was secretary at our local cement plant in Cape Girardeau. She lived on William Street, which is a main artery going through town. And about nine-thirtyish on [a] Sunday night . . ." Smith trailed off as Echols slipped him a note. He murmured a response.

"Do you know where William Street is?" Smith asked.

"I think so. Yeah," Krajcir said.

Smith pointed out that if he'd gone to Saint Francis Medical Center, he'd been on William Street. Krajcir didn't argue the point.

"She came home and went in her home. Someone was waiting. She was sexually assaulted and murdered. Do you remember that?" Smith's voice stayed steady, but it had taken on a more intense tone.

"No," Krajcir said.

"Did you know that lady?" Smith asked.

"No."

Smith described the exact address, a main intersection, William Street and West End, the house on the right, moving away from the river.

"I have no idea," Krajcir said flatly.

"Did you know anyone on William Street?" Smith asked.

"No," Krajcir said.

"Ever been in anyone's house in Cape Girardeau?" Smith asked.

"I don't know anybody from Cape Girardeau," Krajcir insisted.

"Did you ever break in anyone's home in Cape Girardeau on William Street?"

"No." Another lie, murmured softly in the confines of the sterile room.

Smith showed him a picture of the house where Mildred Wallace lived. Krajcir didn't care.

"This is the back of the home. Bathroom window.

Bathroom. Back of the house. Bathroom window. Any of those look familiar?" Smith pressed.

"No."

"So you deny knowing the lady, ever being there at the home. Are you familiar with DNA analysis?" the detective repeated.

This time Krajcir nodded his head slowly and muttered in the affirmative.

Smith handed him the lab report indicating that an impression of Krajcir's palm had been matched to one lifted from the back window of the house in the photographs.

Krajcir didn't say anything for a moment.

"What went wrong in that case? What did she do?" Echols asked, ignoring the long train of denials.

"I don't want to talk about it," Krajcir said stubbornly. As Echols continued to nudge, Krajcir seemed to be searching for a response that might halt the long line of questions he wasn't willing to answer.

"I mean, we know what happened in the Sheppard case, we talked about that. There was a reason. And in this case, there had to be a reason, too," Echols said.

Smith told him that the victim had been sixty-five years old when she died.

"I mean, whatever this evil part of you that comes out during these things, there . . . seems to be something that . . . sets that off and . . . I mean it's not much of a defense, but we'd like to know what happened . . . These other cases you didn't kill them. But in that case you killed her . . . What happened that motivated that?" Echols kept on relentlessly, despite Krajcir's apparent reluctance.

"I'm not going to talk about it," Krajcir insisted.

Echols wondered if any of Krajcir's brothers had ever come to visit him in Cape Girardeau or Carbondale. Krajcir was one step ahead of him.

"As far as I know, neither one of them has ever done anything like that," he answered.

"Do you have any questions, Tim, about what's gonna happen with this case?" Smith asked.

Krajcir had no idea what they had planned, and despite his refusal to admit to the crimes, the idea that anyone else might take credit seemed to displease him. Smith informed him that a meeting with the prosecutor in Cape Girardeau was scheduled for the following day. It was a capital case, and he wanted Krajcir to be aware of that. Elements existed in the case that would compel the prosecutor to seek the death penalty. Smith said he would return in a few days, armed with an arrest warrant listing the charges.

"I can't make any deals with you or anything like that. I'm not even gonna profess that I can even begin to do that, but I can certainly relay something from you to our prosecutor. Now . . . it's a death penalty case. And it will be filed as such. And my recommendation . . . I know if I were in your position I would want to . . . think about some way that I could negotiate my way out of that. It's your decision," Smith said.

"Well . . ." Krajcir hesitated.

"I mean, these families have been victims for a long time. And you know . . . you say we're dealing with two different Tims. I can respect that, you know. You've done a lot of good things. You have," Smith said.

The one good thing Timothy Krajcir had done was keep himself off the streets all these years. No one in the room had any doubt about that.

"You recognized yourself that the other Tim is a dangerous person. That is commendable. And I think the families will appreciate that. That's part of it, but they also need something from you, you know . . ." Smith said.

"They deserve that," Echols said.

"And I think I'm done talking and I'll take whatever comes," Krajcir said. He knew his rights.

"Do you have any defense of that?" Echols couldn't let it drop just yet.

"No, I . . . like I said, I've been twisted since I was a little kid and now it's just catching up with me," Krajcir argued.

Echols urged him to admit his guilt, and try to negotiate the best deal he could.

"Well, maybe if I had a life, you know. But I don't have any life. I haven't had a life for twenty years," Krajcir declared.

It was true, and neither detective knew how to respond.

"I—" Smith began.

Krajcir cut him off. "This is no life."

"I know," Smith answered.

"I'm ready to give up this life tomorrow. I mean, I don't want to spend another thirty years in here. I mean I have . . . like now, I have to find things from one . . . what should I look forward to tomorrow? Why do I want to wake up tomorrow? I mean I'm doing this the last two years trying to fight that kind of depression," Krajcir said sadly.

"I know it's a sad situation," Smith said.

"So . . . so . . . it's all in here. If I die tomorrow, I don't care," Krajcir said.

Smith decided to level with him.

"You've done a lot of bad things on earth. There's no doubt about that. A lot of bad things. To a lot of different people. And you've also hurt yourself in return, but now when it's all meeting you head-on, it may be an opportunity for you to stand up and admit to that. Admit to yourself. That you done all those bad things. And try to give yourself some peace, too," Smith said.

The speech was eloquent, and poignant, but Krajcir rejected Smith's advice.

"I've already made peace with myself. I'm just waiting for death," he said.

Smith looked at him hard. "Are you sure about that?"

Echols asked why, if he'd truly found peace, was he so unwilling to share it with his victims?

"No . . . no . . . I'm done talking now," Krajcir said. "I'm not gonna talk about any of that stuff anymore. Whatever happens, happens, but if I die tomorrow, I don't care."

"So you don't care about families that are living and—" Smith said.

"Don't care. About anything. Pretty much," Krajcir answered, his tone level.

Smith expressed pity for him. He'd spent a good chunk of his career working these cases, and he'd spoken with a lot of friends and family members of the victims. He lived and worked in Cape Girardeau. He knew the toll this wave of crime had taken on the community, even if Krajcir didn't want to acknowledge it.

"It's still fresh in their mind[s] after all these years." Smith wanted him to know that.

"Tim, it doesn't stop with that case either. It just keeps going. There are other cases. And there's a lot of people hurting out there, and you're the only one that can bring closure and help them through that. I mean, once again, what's left? What's left with your life . . ." Echols's voice trailed off as the detective tried to find a tactful way to put it.

"After this I'm . . . I'm not gonna have any life, so . . ." Krajcir let the thought dangle.

Echols asked him if he'd truly known it would all catch up with him one day. Krajcir said yes, he'd always thought it might.

Echols said he wasn't just doing a job here. He had a real ache to know what had happened, and what drove Krajcir to kill in these situations instead of just rape and hurt.

If he knew the answer Echols was looking for, Krajcir pointed out, none of it would have happened. He didn't know.

"We're just doing our jobs and I . . . I appreciate you for recognizing it," Echols said.

They intended to take Krajcir back through every case they'd dug up in which his involvement was suspected. He didn't voice any objections, but he didn't seem thrilled about it either.

"And, Tim, I have no doubt there's more, but this is what we're aware of right now," Smith told him.

Leslie's first assault was initiated in the Wal-Mart parking lot in 1977. Also that month, a young college girl named Sheila Cole had been abducted from the same parking lot one early evening. She'd been picking up some photographs from the store. Smith showed Krajcir a photograph of Sheila's blue Chevy sitting in the lot.

"The following day she was found murdered in a restroom, just across the bridge from Cape Girardeau in Illinois. She was shot twice," Smith said.

"Show him the last one," Echols said.

Smith held up a crime scene photo taken at the Parsh residence.

"August 1977. Mary Parsh lived at 612 Koch Street, which is about four blocks south of William Street, going toward the West Park Mall, that you're aware [of]. You know where that is. You said it before, right?" Smith asked.

"Shopping center?" Krajcir questioned.

Smith was grateful for even that slight acknowledgment. "Shopping center," he agreed. "She comes home one night with her daughter, age twenty-eight, Brenda, to this home. Her husband was in the hospital. Mary picks her daughter up at the airport. They drive directly home. Someone's waiting on them. They were found on a Monday. That was Friday night. They were found on a Monday. Laying side by side on her bed. Hands bound behind their backs with an electrical cord. Each shot in the head. In January of 1982, just down the street, a fifty-eight-year-old widow of three years, Marjorie Call, came to her home, where she lived alone. That's a photograph of the back of that home. She was found the following morning by her brother. She had been strangled on her bed. These cases have created a lot of victims, Tim, over the years," Smith finished.

"And . . . and there's still victims. In all . . . [as] this progressed through the years, there's still lots of victims. There's lots of people out there who deserve to have some closure to this," Echols said.

By way of referencing another case, Smith asked Krajcir if he'd ever been to Scott City.

Krajcir said no, he hadn't.

"This little girl, she was . . . I think nineteen years old. Working at a gas station. Ten-thirty, eleven-thirty in the morning, she was abducted, four hundred and fifty dollars missing from the business. Never been seen again. Not heard of," Smith said.

The date Cheryl Ann Scherer disappeared had been April 17, Easter Sunday, of 1977. Krajcir had been out of jail on bond then. He insisted he'd never even been in Scott City.

Smith reminded him about the forensic testing they'd done in the Wallace case. He and Echols told him they were confident the results would implicate him, rendering his denials of the crime ridiculous and punching holes in his credibility. In a lot of the crimes, officers had collected semen samples, and they were working on getting them tested also.

"You just have nothing to say about those cases. There's nothing we can tell the victims on your behalf."

Echols couldn't believe how strongly Krajcir was clinging to his innocence, even in the face of physical evidence.

"Is there anything you'd ever want to tell the victims?
Personally? If you had an opportunity? Could you do
that? Or would you do that?" Smith asked.

"I'm not talking. I . . . no, there ain't no sense in me
talking anymore," Krajcir said.

"Okay. There's even another one. Paducah, Kentucky.
June 22, 1981. A lady by the name of Anna Brantley. She
was seventy-four years old. The suspect went through the
back door." Echols had part of the report in his hand, and
he glanced down at it, unfamiliar with the facts.

"Strangled or asphyxiated, one way or the other. [Did]
you go to Paducah any?" Echols asked.

"No." Krajcir had already told them he was done
talking.

"Never been to Paducah?" Echols pressed.

"Well, I've been to the hospital there, but I've never . . .
never been there other than that," Krajcir said.

Smith tried again to offer the chance to negotiate.

"So you're not interested in any type of cooperation?
Talking about other cases and trying to . . . negotiate
anything? The reason I ask that . . . my prosecutor—"

Krajcir cut him off.

"Just because I . . . I don't think it would make any
difference. Even . . . if I wanted to cooperate. Even if I
wanted to explain. Say anything about anything. I don't
think it would make any difference."

Krajcir didn't see how any explanation offered by a
killer could affect the outcome of the cases. He didn't

think apologies would give solace to anyone at this point. He'd done so many horrible things. Nothing he could give his victims' loved ones at this point would sway authorities from seeking the death sentence. How could it?

"You don't think you could negotiate yourself out of that. Is that what you're saying?" Smith asked.

"Yes."

Echols asked if he really wanted to make a deal, to bargain his way out of death by lethal injection.

"I don't [have] a . . . death wish, but I don't have a life either, so . . ." Krajcir said.

"So . . . it really doesn't matter what happens to you from here on out, is that what you're saying?" Echols guessed.

Pretty much, Krajcir said.

"Salvage something out of it. Help us with these families. Tim . . . it's the right thing to do. You know that . . . What else is left? . . . They deserve this. I mean if . . . you don't really care what happens to you, then at least do that for them. At least be able to stand up and take responsibility and put their minds at ease," Echols concluded. Slowly, the detectives were wearing Krajcir down, and both cops could sense his resolve weakening.

"Nah . . ." Krajcir said, but it wasn't the same curt refusal they'd grown accustomed to hearing during this interview.

Smith threw his ace onto the table.

"If you had some assurance that you could negotiate yourself out of the death penalty, what would you think about that?" he asked.

"I would think about it. That's all I'm gonna say. But I don't think that's gonna happen, though," Krajcir said.

Smith might be able to do that right now, Echols informed him. He could make one phone call, and make the offer, but they needed full disclosure. He could not stress that enough. They weren't interested in bits and pieces, in dribbles of information. Anything less than brutal honesty and any possibility of striking a deal vanished. The two detectives wanted Krajcir to know that.

"[Smith] can't make any promises, but he has a phone number in his pocket that he needs to call," Echols said.

"It's not something that hasn't been done before, you know," Smith added. "I'm a cop. I can't sit here and tell you exactly what's going to happen. There will be certain points that you will have to meet. I do know that. And one of them is total disclosure. Everything. Today. Not some other day, but today. You know. The death penalty's kind of like . . . the DNA results. It either is or it isn't, you know. You can't file one day and then suddenly decide I'm gonna take it away and then file it again the next day . . . It's so important."

Cape Girardeau's prosecutor, Morley Swingle, was waiting for Smith's phone call. The ball was in Krajcir's court, but Swingle was calling the shots. The ultimate decision was in his lap.

Krajcir agreed to listen to Swingle's offer. He told Smith to go ahead and make the phone call. They took a break while Smith went outside to use the phone.

Krajcir got a drink of water and used the restroom.

Twenty-two minutes later, the interview resumed.

Echols hit Krajcir with the bad news first. Smith had been unable to reach Swingle, so they had nothing to offer at this time. It was up to Krajcir whether he continued to talk.

"Yeah. . . . I need some time just . . ."

"Need some time to think?" Smith asked.

Krajcir nodded slightly.

"Okay. That's fair enough. I understand that," Echols said.

"We've thrown a lot of things at you for you to consider. And . . . it is our understanding that once we . . . get hold of the prosecutor . . . you might be willing to discuss these cases. The case[s] we've talked about?" Echols wanted to be clear.

He needed to think about everything, Krajcir said.

Echols asked him about the Illinois cases. He went on the record saying they had no intention of prosecuting Krajcir for any of those old cases. All they wanted was closure. He offered to make any accommodation that Krajcir requested.

"Try to give me at least a couple of days to think this thing through," Krajcir said.

Echols asked him if there was anything solid they could take back to Swingle.

Krajcir stammered incoherently.

"Got your head spinning, huh?" Echols could only imagine.

"Yeah," Krajcir said quietly.

Before concluding the interview, Echols went over the Illinois rape cases again. There were the two that occurred in Marion and the Johnston City assault. Then there was the one that took place on North Almond Street in Carbondale. Echols offered him absolution of the entire string of sexual assaults. Krajcir said that he understood the circumstances.

At 12:01 in the afternoon on November 14, 2007, Echols turned off the video recorder, concluding his and Smith's first encounter with Krajcir.

Krajcir's fate hung in the balance as with shackled feet, he shuffled back to his cell.

Chapter 10

Bargaining

Cape Girardeau prosecutor Morley Swingle had no intention of sparing the life of Timothy Krajcir. He planned on seeking the death penalty for the murder of Mildred Wallace. The man had lain in wait for a sixty-five-year-old woman to walk through the door of her own home, then brutally raped her, tied a blindfold over her eyes, bound her hands, and shot her in the head. Swingle felt that Krajcir deserved to die.

A russet-haired, tireless litigator known for his colorful wordplay during closing arguments, Swingle had established a reputation as a tough prosecutor. He sought tough sentences, and this was no exception, but he knew he needed to speak with Wallace's family first. Ultimately, it would be their call whether or not Timothy Krajcir would live if convicted.

The families of Sheila Cole, Mary and Brenda Parsh, Margie Call, and Mildred Wallace had become very close over the years. They leaned on one another for support, and that was important right now. On Thanksgiving Day 2007, Swingle spoke with each family by turn. He explained that they had a suspect, a strong suspect, in the killings. The man was already safely incarcerated for another crime, and would likely never see the light of day.

They'd matched a palm print, and they had a solid DNA match in the Wallace case. Not foolproof, but strong. Swingle didn't want to bargain with Krajcir; he wanted to prosecute him. He knew he could win this case. He'd won murder convictions on much less physical evidence, and the man in these cases had just pleaded guilty to a very similar murder. Prosecuting one murder case was selfish, however, when he could clear up five long-unsolved ones, and he had to consider *all* of the victims in these crimes.

Swingle told the Wallace family, what remained of it, about the interview that a Cape Girardeau detective had just done with Krajcir, and that Krajcir had expressed a possible willingness to speak about the other murders if he had reassurance that he would not receive a death sentence.

Later, the family members said they hadn't even needed to think about it. Sparing Krajcir's life seemed a small price to pay for the closure they'd so desperately sought for so long. They would rather know the truth than seek vengeance, in the end. Mildred Wallace's niece said she couldn't see denying other families the possibility of having that precious closure just to see her aunt's killer put to death. Vengeance wouldn't bring her back.

That week, Swingle drafted a letter to the Illinois public defender who'd been assigned to Krajcir. He informed her that he planned to prosecute Krajcir for first-degree murder in the killing of Mildred Wallace in 1982. The suspect's DNA and his palm print had been found at her home. Swingle would file charges within the next month or so. He wanted to let her know so she could best advise her client.

Krajcir's DNA sample was currently being tested against samples taken from other cold case rapes and murders in the area within the same time frame. It seemed probable that Krajcir had committed multiple murders in Cape Girardeau.

In the letter, Swingle informed Krajcir's attorney that Missouri was one of the more efficient states in the country when it came to carrying out the death penalty. He had gotten a death penalty in four felonies, and one of those criminals had already been executed.

He had intended to seek the death penalty in prosecuting the Wallace homicide, Swingle wrote. He'd met during the past week with the families of the victims in Cape Girardeau, however, and they informed him that they wanted to know the truth about the crimes committed there. They had convinced him to not seek the death penalty if there was a possibility of getting a thorough and complete statement from her client as to the details of the commission of each of the particular crimes.

Swingle wasn't at all interested in listening to a convicted killer confess to something he didn't do in order to receive a sweet deal. He only wanted the truth, and it had to be complete.

He would want a separate statement, at least ten to

twenty pages long, to go along with each crime. The length was specified in the letter because Swingle wanted Krajcir and his attorney to understand what he was looking for. He expected every detail, from the planning and preparation stages of each crime through to its conclusion, and he wanted details that would convince him that Krajcir was really the killer. Swingle made clear that he'd be looking for the kind of small, seemingly unimportant details that police would be able to verify. The possibility of getting the truth was the only reason he'd even consider waiving the death penalty.

Swingle also wanted Krajcir to take and pass a polygraph test for each individual statement. He didn't want a false confession, nor did he want a sanitized confession. These had been brutal crimes, and the confessions had better reflect that.

Part of the agreement involved getting a cooperative guilty plea out of Krajcir. Swingle was willing to agree to a sentence of life without parole in each of the murder charges he anticipated filing.

If Krajcir violated the agreement by getting caught in a lie, Swingle would pursue the death penalty in the Wallace case or any of the others. Swingle wouldn't use any of Krajcir's statements against him in case the deal fell through and the case went to trial, unless of course he needed to impeach something Krajcir said on the stand.

The agreement extended to any crimes Krajcir admitted committing in Cape Girardeau County, even those that weren't yet on the radar. There was a push to get the information about the Cape Girardeau cases out of Krajcir before December 10, 2007, the day he was slated to plead guilty to killing Deborah Sheppard.

On December 3, Detectives Echols and Smith again made the trip to Big Muddy to interview Krajcir. This time, he expected them. Armed with Morley Swingle's letter, Smith had every intention of succeeding in getting a confession.

Krajcir started things off by requesting a root beer. Everyone else was drinking coffee. It was about six-thirty in the evening.

"I've already had about three cups of coffee. I'm going to have a buzz here in a little while," Krajcir said.

Smith pointed out that there was probably more caffeine in the root beer.

The guard offered to fetch Krajcir his can of soda. Krajcir responded that the guard might as well take his time. He planned on being there for a while.

"Well, just get comfortable. That's the most important part." Echols seemed nervous about the whole affair.

"All right," Krajcir said, not seeming jittery at all.

Again, on the tape, Echols and Smith identified themselves and stated their purposes. Smith provided Krajcir with a Miranda warning.

Krajcir chose not to have an attorney present during this interview, and he signed a waiver to that effect. He had, however, requested Echols's presence during the first interview. Echols had already told him that he couldn't answer his questions about the possibility of extradition.

Smith went ahead and read Krajcir the letter Swingle had written to the public defender in Illinois. At its conclusion, the two detectives chattered nervously between themselves for a moment. Everyone in the room, including the warden, was well aware of what was at stake.

Krajcir appeared eager to get started. Or maybe he was just relieved that the waiting had ended, and the day he'd suspected would eventually come had at last arrived. He was ready to talk.

"Any particular place you want to begin, Tim?" Smith asked.

"Uh . . . let's begin where I started. When I first raped Leslie."

There, he'd finally said it. The truth that had lain hidden from the residents of Cape Girardeau for thirty years was finally going to come out.

Smith took a breath. "Okay. Do you recall what . . . year that was by any chance?"

"'Seventy-seven, I think," Krajcir replied.

"How do you remember that to be 1977?" Smith wanted to know.

"I know I'd been out [of prison] eight or nine months," he said. Krajcir had been in prison so often he tended to use it as a chronological marker.

"I had a relationship with this one gal I knew. And at that time we broke up . . . it was at that point that I made . . . probably the most stupidest [mistake] in my life, which was to go out and . . . rape again," Krajcir said.

Smith murmured an acknowledgment, but didn't want to interrupt now that he'd finally gotten to this point.

"So that night or [in] a couple of days, in there somewhere I drove down . . . I didn't want to [do] nothing around Carbondale. I was living there," Krajcir went on slowly.

"Was your girlfriend from Carbondale or was she from Missouri?" Smith asked.

"Well, . . . no, she was . . . she was a married gal. That I had met." Krajcir almost seemed ashamed.

"Okay," Smith said.

"I don't think her name is really necessary. Anyway, I was in a depressing . . . depressing type mood, which usually triggers me going out and doing something. And I drove to Cape Girardeau. And I said to myself, the first . . . I went to Mohr Value, I think it was then, or Wal-Mart right there," Krajcir said. He recalled it being a rainy night. "I said to myself the first good-looking gal that comes up there by herself, I'm going to assault."

"Where were you parked?" Smith asked.

"I was parked in the parking lot."

"Okay."

"Just waiting," Krajcir added.

Darkness had already fallen, he continued. He guessed it was probably around eight or maybe eight-thirty, but he couldn't recall what time of year it had been.

"Was summer over? Was it summertime? Winter? Do you recall how you were dressed?" Smith pressed.

"No, probably a . . . baseball hat . . . dungarees and a shirt at the time," Krajcir said.

"I understand. Some of those little details can be hard to remember," Smith sympathized.

"Thirty years ago. I'll try. And . . . I think I had a knife. I knew she was the first one that pulled up and . . ." Krajcir thought he was lucky that the first woman to come along was as attractive as Leslie.

"Had she already been in the store or . . . was she

coming back? Back to get in her car? Do you recall that?" Smith asked.

"I think she was coming back to get in her car," Krajcir answered, but he didn't sound certain.

"Was she alone?" Smith asked.

"No, she had her daughter with her."

Smith asked him for a description of the lady he was talking about.

"It was a young black woman. Just . . . pretty . . . pretty attractive, from what I could see. Like I say it was dark. And I . . . got out of my car and she was opening the door and I went and threatened her with the knife. At first we got into her car. And then . . . I . . . I . . . didn't want to do anything there, so we got in my car. And I was threatening her all the time with violence if she didn't do what I said. And . . . we just drove around. I don't know where I was going."

"So you drove her car?"

"No, my car," Krajcir corrected him.

"You drove your car. What kind of car did you have at that time?" Smith asked.

"Uh . . .'69 Dodge Coronet. Blue. Four-door. Like I say, I don't know where I was going. We drove around for a while. It started to rain. And we came into a dark area."

Smith wanted to know where the little girl had been sitting in the car during this drive.

"She was in the backseat," Krajcir answered.

"Sitting up? Laying down?"

"I think she was laying down in the backseat."

"Do you recall how old she was?"

"Four or five. Something like that maybe, she was

kind of small. I don't think she really knew what was going on . . . so I drove to this dark area."

Smith murmured an affirmative response.

"And it was raining. I know it was raining. And I told [Leslie] to take her clothes off. And she says . . . rather than have intercourse with you . . . would you let me do you orally? And I said okay. And, uh . . . she was doing me orally and I told her to stop. And I was gonna have intercourse with her . . ."

Smith murmured again as if they were discussing the weather or the St. Louis Cardinals. That was Krajcir's trademark, the ability to appear normal even when he was discussing acts that rendered him criminally insane.

"Got in the position for intercourse, but we never . . . did have intercourse . . . I stopped. And got up. I think she put her clothes back on and I took her back to the . . . uh . . . Mohr Value. She got in her car and I took off. That was pretty much [the] first one . . . the first time," Krajcir said.

"What did you say to her when you first approached her on the parking lot? Do you recall?" Smith asked.

"Oh, I'll . . . I know I threatened her, but . . . I couldn't tell you." Krajcir's memory was fuzzy after thirty years.

Smith murmured again, letting Krajcir know he was paying attention to every detail the other man pulled from his memory.

"I know I had a knife. The knife was open. And I told her I wasn't gonna . . . I don't want to hurt you. Just do what I say," Krajcir recalled.

"When you left the parking lot, where was she sitting in the vehicle?" Smith asked.

"She was in the front seat."

"Was she sitting up?"

"I don't think she was. I think she was . . . she was laying down."

"Do you know where her head was placed at that time?"

Here was where the detectives had the advantage. In the 1970s and 1980s, the rape crimes were not covered by the news media as extensively as murder cases. If a story appeared in a newspaper at all, it would have been short. In the case of Leslie's assaults, Smith had a plethora of details that only the real perpetrator could know. This gave him a solid way to gauge Krajcir's honesty.

"I'm not sure. Not sure," Krajcir said in answer to Smith's question about where her head had been.

"Did you take anything from her? Personal property?" Smith asked. "Did you look in her purse?"

"Before I left, I tried to bribe her. I gave her some money," Krajcir said.

"Do you know how much?"

"It was like a twenty-dollar bill or something like that. I was gonna give her more but I . . . I didn't have it. And I think I apologized to her even. That was the first time I had done anything. Since I'd been released. And, uh . . . I don't think I felt too good about it. I remember I did give her the money. And then she said something about . . . all of this . . . I think it was a sarcastic remark, but you know, and then I took off after that."

"Was the little girl upset at that time? Do you recall? What was she doing?"

"I don't remember her being upset."

"What kind of threat do you recall making to her?"

"You mean when I left?" Krajcir asked.

Smith murmured an inaudible response to the question.

"Well . . . uh . . . I really don't remember making a threat to her when I left," Krajcir said.

"Okay, do you recall how long you'd been in Cape Girardeau that night before you picked her up?"

Krajcir guessed he hadn't sat in the parking lot longer that a half hour to forty-five minutes tops before he spotted Leslie and her child. He'd chosen Wal-Mart's lot, he said when Smith asked how he'd made his selection, because he figured that's where most women would go shopping.

The rest of his decision was pure chance, he recalled, nothing really more tangible than a whim.

"When you left the parking lot that night with her . . . you say her head was on . . . your leg I believe, if I recall correctly. Did she, uh . . . perform oral sex on you as you were driving? Or do you recall that?" Smith asked.

Krajcir didn't remember.

"You don't recall or she didn't?"

"She didn't."

Smith asked if Echols had any questions about the incident.

"You went to Cape Girardeau with the sole purpose of committing a rape?" Echols wanted to know.

That had been pretty much the way it had gone, Krajcir agreed.

"I mean, you said you drove out of Carbondale, because you were living in Carbondale, so you didn't want to do anything in Carbondale?" Echols pressed.

That pretty well summed it up. Krajcir could present no other motive for being in Cape Girardeau that night.

"I think that was the first time," he said.

"That was your first time over there?" Smith asked.

"Yeah," Krajcir said, then amended his statement. "Well, it wasn't the first time I was in Cape, but it was first time . . ."

"The first time you'd committed a crime there?" Smith asked.

"Yes."

"You had driven the ambulance over there prior to that point?" Echols asked.

Krajcir thought he'd been there maybe three or four times. All of those were trips to either Southeast or Saint Francis hospitals. He then told the detectives about the second time he'd assaulted Leslie. He'd seen her come out of a store at the West Park Mall. Pure curiosity had drawn him to that parking lot.

All he'd hoped for had been an attractive woman. He'd gotten Leslie. At first, he'd had absolutely no idea she wasn't a total stranger. He followed her.

As he'd approached her house on that freezing-cold day, he didn't recognize her. Thinking back, as he relayed the story to Echols and Smith, he said there was a possibility that she'd recognized him when he appeared so suddenly in the darkness as she went to wring out her mop.

"Did you ever remove the bandanna the night you were in Leslie's residence?" Smith asked him.

"I may have, but I . . . I don't remember for sure," Krajcir replied.

226

"Did it ever come to you that night that you realized that she was likely the lady that you . . . uh . . . raped back in 1977?" Smith asked.

"I think I might've . . . had a little suspicious after I was there for a while."

"Do you recall saying anything to her about that when you were there?" Smith wanted to know.

Krajcir didn't recall.

The detectives hurried Krajcir through the interview in order to get to the slayings of the Parsh women.

"Do you recall what the house looked like?" Smith asked.

"It was kind of a small house," Krajcir said.

Smith asked if he knew the color. It had been too dark to tell, Krajcir answered.

He remembered that there wasn't a garage, and that the woman he'd gone to stalk at the ranch-style house owned a big, long car, like a Cadillac-style sedan. He couldn't remember the specific make or model of the beast, though.

"Anyway, I looked in the window. I didn't see . . . see anybody or anything," Krajcir went on.

He'd peeped through a bedroom window in the back of the house.

He decided to wait a week and then return. He planned to assault her then. It had been a Friday night, he thought, when he drove back to Cape Girardeau and parked near the Koch Street residence.

"Can we jump back just a bit?" Smith asked suddenly.

"Okay," Krajcir said.

"On that night you were there, peeping through the window, did you . . . did you see the lady?" Smith questioned.

Krajcir had. She'd beaten him home when he followed her, and was already in the house when he walked around to the rear. She was alone when he looked through her window.

Then he backpedaled a bit. During the course of the interview, Krajcir had struggled to recall details of the horrors he'd inflicted on women over the past twenty years. He knew the importance of furnishing the state with those details. Swingle had made this abundantly clear in his letter to Krajcir's attorney, which had been read to Krajcir over and over. Their deal to waive the penalty depended largely on the accuracy of the old man's memory.

"Let me think a . . . second . . . maybe even the first time she might not have been home. Or I was around there and she might have come home. While I was there and then I looked in the window. I'm not . . . not real sure about that. I know the second time, she wasn't home." Krajcir plowed on through the details of the incident, struggling with his memory.

"Was it dark each time you were there?" Smith asked.

Krajcir replied that it had been. He remembered that the date had been sometime in August of 1977, because he'd had a friend's wedding scheduled that same week.

Smith allowed him to continue with his description of what had transpired the second time he'd gone to the Parsh home.

"I broke the back window. It was a window that didn't go up and down, you had to crank it. And it came this way," Krajcir said, gesturing outward.

"It pulls out from the house?"

"Yeah. That's how I entered. And when—" Krajcir began, but Smith interrupted.

"How did you get in that window?"

He'd crawled inside, a feat that was easier said than done, considering what a big guy Krajcir had been back then.

Smith asked if the window had already been opened.

"No . . . well, I smashed the window. And opened it," Krajcir said.

He thought he remembered putting his coat up against the window to protect his arm and then smashing the glass.

"And then once I got inside, there was glass there. I think I tried to hide it. And just . . . just . . . I was waiting for her to come home. I think maybe . . . maybe thirty minutes or less. She . . . she came home. She had her daughter with her. So I didn't know this was gonna . . . gonna happen. But anyway, I was already in the house."

Krajcir faltered when he talked about Brenda's unexpected presence. Here was a man who clearly did not like surprises. He obviously expected events to unfold in a neat, orderly fashion.

"And they came in and I think they were talking. Went to this room where there were two bunk beds. And that's where I . . . accosted them. Brought them out there and I think they was both kneeled down and . . ." Krajcir said.

Smith wanted to know if he'd been armed the night he'd gone to the Parsh house.

"I had that .38 with me. That I got . . . that I stole in the burglary," Krajcir said.

"You don't remember if it was a Charter Arms? A Smith and Wesson? Or . . . or whatever?" Smith pressed.

Krajcir didn't remember what kind of gun it had been. He thought it may have been a Smith & Wesson, but he couldn't say for sure. He'd lost it years ago. He said he knew it had definitely been the same gun he'd stolen from the burglary in Carbondale.

Smith understood his hesitancy in giving some of the details, like the make of gun. A slipup here, speaking up before he was certain his memory was reliable, could ultimately cost him his life.

"I had them kneel down there in front. I took them into the . . . I know I think I just had them kneel down there to threaten them," Krajcir said.

"Do you recall what you said to them?" Smith asked.

"Do what I say or you know, I'm gonna have to hurt somebody. That's . . . that was my usual . . . usual thing." It was a phrase that the two detectives would hear over and over.

He didn't recall them saying anything to him in return. They might have been paralyzed with fear.

He made them both undress and asked them for oral sex. They disrobed and sat down side by side on the bed.

"I didn't do anything with the mother," Krajcir said.

Smith asked if he meant that particular moment, or that he'd never done anything with her the entire night.

Krajcir said he hadn't touched the mother at all.

"You didn't touch the mother. Okay," Smith acknowledged.

"Well, I think I caressed her a few times whenever

I . . . when I laid her on the bed. But I didn't have any sex with her at all. Or oral or intercourse or nothing."

The two women were scared. Krajcir could see that they weren't going to put up a fight. They followed all of his instructions and went along with all of his orders.

Krajcir thought he remembered performing oral sex on Brenda. A little bit, he said.

"I did not have intercourse with her. And I . . . I don't think I ejaculated either. I'd uh . . . had . . . I had a climax but it . . . like a dry climax," he said, his tone placid.

Smith murmured a response.

"I don't think there was any semen," Krajcir said.

Echols interrupted to ask if Krajcir had bound their hands while he assaulted Brenda. Krajcir didn't recall whether they had been bound yet or not. He remarked that he didn't believe they had.

"To be truthful . . . I . . . it's like fifty-fifty . . . I'm not a hundred percent sure of it. I think I did. I think I tied them up with something, but I can't remember what it was."

Smith tried to jog his memory without giving too many facts away.

"Do you ever recall anywhere where you would have happened to have cut an electrical cord . . . ?" He let his voice trail off.

This did the trick.

"Yes."

"Maybe plugged in?" Smith pressed.

"Yes, yes," Krajcir said. He remembered now.

It could have been at that point that he tied the women up.

"Yeah. I might have tied them up with a lamp cord," he recalled.

The cord had rubbed a hole in his knife, he realized. Then was when that had happened.

When he'd cut the cord with his small knife, he'd gotten a nasty shock.

"I might have . . . the same thing happened in a . . . another rape that I did, but I can't remember for sure. That wasn't in Cape Girardeau, it was in Pennsylvania. Okay . . . tie them up in bed," he said.

Smith asked if he'd remembered having them tied up with their hands behind their backs.

"I think I had them lying on their stomachs."

Krajcir recalled covering them up.

"I think the daughter was on the right-hand side of the bed and the mother on the left," he said.

That was just how it had worked out.

Krajcir interrupted the questioning at that moment. He felt it was important—important to him, at least— that they understand what had been running through his head at this particular moment in time.

"It's directly related to what happens after. Uh . . . 1963 they sent me to uh . . . Menard Psychic. At that time, I was eighteen. Probably the worst place anybody could send any youngster. 'Cause at the time it was filled with the criminally insane. Every kind of sexual deviate that you can imagine. A couple of guys off of death row who were like crazy. I'm talking about the whole population was that kind of mix. Criminally insane. And I'm not . . . I don't mean normal people, I mean they were criminally insane. And it was probably the worst two years of my life, the first two years I was there. Anyway, they kept me there for about five years. When I left there I was full of rage and anger, it was unbelievable. Uh . . . the first couple of years were full of humiliations. Uh . . . if it wouldn't have been for sports, coming in at that time, really coming in, I would have probably gone crazy. I think sports probably were the only thing that kept me sane all of these years. Anyway, while there, I would talk to some of the guys in the yard . . . Do you remember Todd Hopkins? He's up in Dixon Psychic for killing his wife and another young girl in Carbondale and somebody else."

Echols knew exactly who he was talking about, and he said so. Hopkins was a well-known criminal. He and Krajcir had been friends.

"He was there for, I think, for assault and battery at that time. He hadn't killed his wife or anybody [yet]. And I remember when we would sit there and talk about different things. I was a youngster, very impressionable. And . . . and one of the things that really stuck on mind, he said, Tim, if you ever do anything, don't leave any witnesses. And for some reason, that just stuck in my brain. All right. And then when I decided to step across the line again in '77 and go back to doing those things . . . it was in my head. But I hadn't done any . . . anything like that because I didn't have the weapons to do it. I didn't know if I could do it. Anyway, when I tied the two ladies up . . ."

"So let me ask you a question about what you just said . . . are you saying that's the first time, 1977, that you committed a murder?" Smith inquired.

"Yes." Krajcir picked up where he'd left off. "Anyway, I got them tied up. At that point I . . . I shot the young girl in the back of the head. I shot the mother in the back of the head."

"You shot the daughter first?" Smith asked.

"Yes. Then I shot the mother in the back of the head. At that time I went around the house, searching for stuff that I . . . I think I . . . went to a room like a den or something."

Krajcir admitted finding a wallet with sixty or seventy dollars in it and taking it.

"From a desk drawer?" Smith clarified.

"Yes, I think so," Krajcir said. "A desk from the den. I went back in the bedroom and the mother was still alive. She was crying next to her daughter. So I fired another shot. And I left." He uttered the statement like he had been talking about brushing his teeth.

"So you shot the daughter, Brenda, first, in the back of the head. [Then you shot her mother.] You went and took money out of the wallet from the den. The mother was still alive. You went back and shot her a second time?" Smith asked.

Krajcir thought he recalled aiming the small pistol straight at the older woman's head.

"Did you ever sexually assault or do anything at all physical with the mother that night?" Smith asked.

"Well, when I was, uh . . . intercourse with her daughter on the bed . . ." Krajcir began. "She was laying right next to me and I may have run my hands over her, but that's it. I didn't have intercourse or oral sex or any of those with her."

"What would have been the reason that you would have had the mother undress?"

"Well, I think it was, uh . . . initially to assault both of them," Krajcir explained as best he could.

Usually, he would commit one assault, have one climax, and that satisfied the urge for a while.

Then he would generally split.

"There was no reason to shoot them," Krajcir admitted. "I mean . . . I don't think they had a good look at my face or anything. But I had that shit in my head."

"Was your face covered?" Smith asked. It was a logical question, and an important one. Every victim who had survived an attack had talked about the man in the blue bandanna, the strip of navy-colored fabric tied around the lower half of his face.

"I know it was when I went in there with the blue bandanna," Krajcir said.

"Did they threaten you that they would call the police?"

"Like right in the middle of all this . . . uh . . . when I was . . . the daughter was giving me oral sex or something if I'm not mistaken, the phone rang. And, uh . . . I think it was her father who was in a hospital on the phone and she talked to her father and I listened in for like two or three minutes. And then he hung up. And I went back to what we were doing."

And there it was, the most revealing detail of the whole confession. Unless he'd been there, Krajcir couldn't have possibly known that Brenda had spoken with her father before she died. The only ones who'd ever even dared think that her killer had listened in on that conversation had been close family members.

Smith wanted to know if Krajcir somehow had known

that Mr. Parsh was in the hospital. Investigators had long suspected that the intruder had some kind of prior knowledge that Mary Parsh would be home alone.

Krajcir would have been in the perfect position, as an ambulance worker, to know that little fact, but he insisted he'd found out through Brenda's conversation with her father. He'd understood that the father was recovering from some kind of surgery.

"Do you recall what Brenda may have said to her father?" Smith asked.

"Oh, man," Krajcir murmured.

"Did you have to threaten her not to say anything to him?" Smith asked.

"I would say that I probably did threaten them not to say anything out of line. I think she said . . . some . . . something like I love you, Daddy or I'll see you tomorrow or . . ." Krajcir said.

Smith asked if he remembered the phone ringing again and Brenda not answering, but Krajcir was uncertain. He remembered her getting up to answer the telephone. At that time, he hadn't yet bound her hands. He didn't tie her up till they were on the bed, he thought.

"How long do you think you'd been in the house when the phone rang? Approximately?" Smith asked.

Krajcir thought it was about twenty-five minutes.

"Was there conversation between you and either of the two? Do you remember them talking to you? Anything that was said? Obviously I would think that they were begging you not to do anything, but . . ." Echols put in.

"Actually, I don't believe they did say very much."

"When you shot the mother the first time, you . . . you thought you shot her in the head?" Echols asked.

"Yes."

"But then you heard her crying when you came back and that's when you shot her the second time?"

Smith wanted to know if he'd moved a pillow that had been lying on the bed.

That was one detail Krajcir was unable to pull from the recesses of his memory.

"When you shot the victims, was it a gun against their head or how was that?" Echols asked.

"I would say it was maybe a foot away. Close, but I don't think I was . . . I'd go like that." Krajcir couldn't remember whether he'd placed anything between the gun and the victims' heads when he fired.

"Did you put a gag on either of them?" Smith asked.

"I don't think so," Krajcir replied. If he had, he didn't remember. He also had no recollection of stuffing anything in the mouths of the victims. At this point, so much time had passed; it was possible such details would never come back to him.

Smith wondered what had happened to Krajcir's gun after that night.

"Well, I kept it. I think I used it one more time."

Smith requested a description of the older woman he'd murdered that night in 1977.

"Dark hair. Maybe a little plump," he said. He thought she was maybe around fifty-one or fifty-two. The daughter had been around twenty-five or twenty-six, very attractive, with long, dark hair.

"Did she tell you anything about her profession, by any chance?" Smith asked.

He'd thought he remembered her saying something about being a writer or something, maybe in St. Louis.

"After their deaths, how long were you in the home?" Smith asked him.

"I'd say no more than five minutes. I didn't hang around . . ." He'd parked his car maybe two blocks from the main intersection near the house. He remembered that the woman had left the house keys in the door, because he'd heard them jangle as he left.

"About what time of the night was that again?" Smith asked.

Krajcir told the detectives everything he could recall about that night. He'd figured it for about ten, and it had been a warm, balmy night. There hadn't been a police car in sight, and he'd never had a glimmer of fear that he'd get caught. At that time, Krajcir hadn't selected any other targets in the neighborhood. He'd done the murder and gone home.

"Most of my targets are random. So, what if it's just, uh . . . faith more than anything, I mean . . ." Krajcir trailed off.

He had specifically targeted Mary Parsh because he'd been under the impression that she lived alone.

Smith told him that one of the victims had suffered a broken tooth and a bruised face. He wanted to know if Krajcir had struck her at any time.

Krajcir answered that right away.

"No, did not. I don't think I ever hit any of my victims. I mean I didn't torture them. I didn't beat them or none of that. Just used a threat with the gun to make them do what I wanted." He was emphatic about this.

"Did you tell them they were gonna die?" Smith asked.

Krajcir didn't think they'd known up until the time he shot them. About five minutes separated the fatal shots. Had Mary Parsh not cried out the way she had, he would have left thinking both women were dead.

Smith began hammering the questions at him in rapid succession.

He asked where the purses had been when Krajcir found them. "Do you know how you looked in the purses?"

"I just opened them up and looked at the wallets and put them back down," Krajcir answered.

"Did you dump anything out anywhere in the residence? Anything of value?"

"I might have dumped the purses, I don't know about . . . but I'm not . . . not sure."

"Do you recall if the lights were on or off, while you were there?"

Krajcir thought they were on in the residence, but he couldn't say for certain. He didn't remember whether he'd had to turn them on or off.

Krajcir said he hadn't paid much attention to the newspapers, but he did recall seeing news broadcast about the crime, about how terrible it had been, but he didn't remember much else about it. He never had any interest in collecting news clippings about any of his crimes.

Smith showed him some photographs of the Parsh house. Recognition flared in Krajcir's eyes.

Krajcir moved on to his assault on Francine, Grace

Larkin's mother, while she was napping, and later, her daughter. He confessed to threatening Francine with the garden rake.

"A sweet old lady. She was so embarrassed she never told nobody or called the police." Krajcir described her as slender, in her midfifties at the time he assaulted her. She'd lived in a fairly beat-up, dilapidated house.

Then he talked about the incident with Grace. That time he'd gone back to the same house, hoping to find her younger sister. He told the detectives every detail he could pull from his memory about that night.

"I think I might have been armed that second time," Krajcir said.

"Well, if . . . there were multiple people in there, how did you secure the others?" Echols asked.

"They were in the front room. It was in the back room," Krajcir said.

"They didn't know you were there?" Echols pressed.

"Yeah, they knew I was there. I just told everybody to stay right there," Krajcir answered.

Echols asked him how many children had been in the room at the time.

He thought he recalled three or four children. He also remembered the grandmother being there, the woman he'd assaulted. She'd been holding a baby.

"That lady you raped the previous time?" Echols asked.

Krajcir hesitated, and Echols clarified his question. "Had her perform oral sex on you?"

Krajcir had intimidated the group until he was confident they'd stay put and be quiet, then he escorted the daughter to the back room.

He threatened her with the gun.

"When you secured them, do you remember how you did that? Whether you had them sit? Lay or whatever?" Smith asked.

"I think they were all sitting . . . on the couch. And Grandma was sitting on the floor. Uh . . . by . . . the window, I think. I didn't hurt nobody and left. Other than the sexual assault."

These were the sorts of crimes that helped convince detectives that Krajcir was telling the truth about what he'd done. First, the victims were still alive, so every detail that Krajcir told police could be verified. Second, those sexual assaults had occurred during a time when rapes rarely made the news. That left an awful lot of details that only the real perpetrator would know.

"Do you recall demanding money or anything?" Smith asked.

"I don't think I did."

He'd entered through the front door.

"Yeah, I think that the teenage girl hadn't been out of the house and, uh . . . when I first got there, I was looking in the window and I heard her say she was gonna run up to the store and get something and come back. So I waited until she came back, and like a minute after she went in the door, I went in the door."

Smith wanted to know how many rapes the man had actually committed in Cape Girardeau.

"Oh . . . there weren't really that many, uh . . . okay,

I burglarized that one little house there, with the two young black girls." Krajcir pointed to the map the detectives showed him. "I went back to the basement . . . basement apartment where the two black girls were. Knocked on the door. I pretended to be a police officer. Showed her . . . I think I had a fake badge or something." That had been a trick of Krajcir's, to flash a phony badge in order to get his victim to open the door. He'd also done it in Pennsylvania to gain entry to Myrtle Rupp's home.

"Do you know where you got that badge?" Smith asked.

"In a department store or something. You can buy them anywhere.

"She let me in. And I had planned to, uh . . . assault her, but she was a pretty smart gal. And, uh . . . as I was getting ready to, uh . . . pull a gun and accost her, she had got up and ran out the door. Went upstairs and got her girl from upstairs to come down with her and I said a few words and then I got out of there as quick as I could get out there.

"She was lucky," he finished.

He went on to describe the assault of the three black ladies who were having the party. "There was another incident; I think this was in '82. I think I remember I had the Plymouth Valiant. It was on the other side of Cape. Wasn't near the post office. There were three black women inside the house."

It had happened over in the south end, the rough side, of Cape Girardeau, he said. He'd scoped out the house first, maybe two weeks before the assault, then followed the home owner back after a shopping trip and spied on her, as had become his routine. He saw an attractive young woman who looked to be in her midtwenties, and appeared to be a single mom with several kids.

"She looked like an easy victim," Krajcir commented.

"I didn't do anything that night. And I think I came back a week . . . a week or two later. Uh . . . I looked in and she wasn't there. There was two other women in there. And, uh . . . usually something like that would . . . I wouldn't even . . . I'd split. But this night I think I . . . pretty sure I was armed. And I went through, uh . . . I'd say it was a little house in the back there was a little screened-in porch."

"Mm-hmm," Smith murmured, encouraging him to move on.

"The door was locked. I couldn't get in the door. So I . . . I think I cut the screen on the back of the porch with my knife and crawled in the back porch. Went in through the kitchen. They were in the front room. I think it was in the summertime, 'cause I remember the door . . . the front door was open. So they was letting the fresh air come in. And there was a . . . before I went in I was . . . I was in the back of the house. This other woman came home. So that made three of them in there."

They were all black females, all fairly young and attractive.

"Another thing I was doing, I don't think I've mentioned this, but while I was locked up I used to imagine sexual fantasies. And I decided when I got out I would do whatever I fantasized about," Krajcir explained.

"If I could . . . two or three women or whatever.

Anyway, I think that's why I went in. I went into the front room. There was three of them sitting on the couch. They were talking and I think they were drinking or something. They had some kind of a . . . whiskey there or something. Anyway, there's a chair over here . . . over here and the couch over there. She took the kids, I think there's two or three of them, and put them in a side room. Closed the door. So they wouldn't see anything. Told them to be quiet and behave themselves. And I had, uh . . . three girls on the couch, had them take their clothes off. I sat there and I was masturbating while they were taking their clothes off. And the woman who lived there, she came over and I asked her to do it, oral sex. She did till I reached climax. And, uh . . . the other two I caressed a couple of times, but . . . but didn't have no sexual relations with either one of them."

He asked if they had any money, and the way he remembered it, they said no. He didn't recall making them dump out their purses one by one and rifling through the contents.

He left then, and he recalled driving his Plymouth, which meant that it had to be 1982. That was the year he had that car, instead of the Dodge.

"Did you have to force that lady to perform oral sex on you or was she agreeable to that?" Smith asked.

"Well, she did, but I . . . I think I put my hand on her head and was putting pressure on her head. She did . . . I don't think she really wanted to." That was putting it mildly.

"But you had the gun, too?" Echols asked.

"Yeah," Krajcir replied.

"Was it displayed at the time?" Smith asked.

"Yes, I believe it was, yes," Krajcir said.

"Bandanna?" Echols inquired.

He wore what he usually had on when he hung around home, blue jeans, a T-shirt, and a hat of some kind, usually a wool cap or ball hat.

"Were these on your days off when you would plan these things?" Echols asked.

"Yeah. Let me think if there were anything else in Cape," he answered.

After a moment's pause, when Krajcir said nothing, Echols announced a break for a few minutes, and clicked off the recording.

When he flicked the switch on the recorder, they resumed the questioning. This time, Krajcir talked about Sheila Cole's murder.

"Now you've already admitted that the handgun was used in the murder of Brenda and Mary Parsh . . . while telling that story you said that you had used it one other time," Echols began.

"Yeah," Krajcir agreed.

"Let's go ahead and maybe talk about that one," Echols said.

"Okay. I think that was a college girl. Young girl that was found on the other side of the river. In a parking lot," Krajcir remembered.

"Where did you happen to see her?" Smith asked.

"The same place I seen Leslie the first time," he said.

"Wal-Mart parking lot in Cape Girardeau?" Smith clarified.

"Yeah. Same exact scenario. Except I took her to my

245

home in Carbondale. Where, uh . . . I took assa . . . assault of her," Krajcir said.

"In whose vehicle?" Smith asked.

The car had been Krajcir's blue Dodge.

"Do you recall what time of the year that was?" Smith asked.

"Probably the late summer. I'm not . . . not sure," he confessed.

Smith clarified that he was talking about 1977. It had actually been November.

"She had parked next to a pretty big truck that had blocked the view from the store. I came around and, uh . . . got her out of the car. Put her in my car. And [went] to Carbondale. I was living in the trailer. I took her in the bedroom," Krajcir said.

"Did you have to tie her hands or anything?" Smith asked.

"No. No. I had her lay—"

"Were you armed?" Smith interrupted.

"Yes. Yes. I had the .38, that same gun . . ."

"Okay, same gun," Smith repeated.

"And she . . . she was laying on the front seat and head in my lap." Krajcir said.

He'd told her to be quiet, and he wouldn't hurt her. He led her out of the Dodge and into the trailer. There, he'd forced her to disrobe. He made her perform oral sex on him.

"That . . . that was all we did. Didn't have intercourse."

"Did you ejaculate?" Smith asked.

"Yes. Yes. It was oral sex."

"In her mouth? Or could it have [gone] somewhere else? Like on her clothing?" Smith asked.

"She might . . . I don't think it was on her clothing. I think she . . . took it in her mouth," Krajcir said. "That was all we did. She got dressed. I told her that I was gonna take her home. We drove back down toward Cape. Stopped there at the park lot, I had to go to that bathroom. She asked if she could go, too."

He thought it was on the right side, the male side, at the little rest area.

"I took her in there. Shot her one time, I think. I might have shot her twice, I'm not sure," Krajcir said. "I think I shot her in the head. Again, it was dark in there."

He thought it had been the side of the head, actually. That was generally where he aimed.

"When you first saw her, what were your intentions . . . with her that night?" Smith asked him then.

"To sexually assault her," Krajcir responded. He never planned to kill anyone.

"Had you already planned to take her back to Carbondale or is that something you . . ."

"That was probably spur of the moment," Krajcir said.

"Why would you risk taking her all the way to Carbondale?" Echols asked.

"When I was in that mode, you don't think."

He knew he had shown the girl the gun initially.

"When I was driving, I might have put it down on the left side of the seat or something. I'm not a hundred percent sure about that."

"Did she leave anything at your apartment? That you may have found later?" Smith asked.

"Not that I'm aware of."

"Did you take any personal items from her?" Smith tried again, hinting that Krajcir might want to think about it awhile longer.

Krajcir told them that he'd put the girl's purse in a trash receptacle outside. "I looked in it, but there was nothing in it."

"When did you decide to kill her?" Smith asked.

"Probably not till I was . . . got close to Cape. I mean [it] was . . . wasn't premeditated."

Smith murmured an agreement.

"It . . . like I said, I had that thing in my head about, you know, no witnesses. And, uh . . . I . . . I was still in that mode. I was in that mode for a couple of years before I finally started to get wear . . . wear out on me, I think."

Krajcir faltered, a common occurrence when he sought to explain his motives.

"Had she done anything that would have irritated you that night?" Smith asked.

"No. No."

"She went along with your wishes?"

"Yes."

"Do you recall anything else she may have said to you [besides] that she was attending college in Cape Girardeau?"

"I think she told me she was sharing an apartment with a couple of, uh . . . girlfriends," he answered.

"What were your intentions when you escorted her to the restroom?" Smith asked.

"I think at that point in time I . . . I decided I was going to kill her."

Smith showed him a photograph of the restroom.

"That looks like the place," Krajcir admitted.

He also held up a picture of Sheila Cole's blue Chevy Nova in the Wal-Mart parking lot.

"That looks like her car," Krajcir said.

"So obviously [there] wasn't a concern of a roommate coming in at that point?" Echols asked.

"Yeah. Even then it was . . . stupid on my part because any one of my friends could have come over. And how could I have explained what was going on? You know? It's just one of those things that . . . that you do without thinking."

Within the next couple of minutes, the conversation wound its way around to the murder of Margie Call.

Krajcir talked about spotting her at the grocery store and following her home.

"It was right around nine or nine-thirty, when she got back to her house," he said.

"So I waited about a week. And went to the house about eight o'clock . . . And I went through, uh . . . I think bedroom or bathroom window. Broke it."

He showed them in the photograph where the window had been located in relation to the residence.

"In the back of the house. Back down this way," he said, pointing.

He remembered that there had been two bathrooms in that house. He'd gone through the whole place, prowling around while waiting for the woman he'd stalked to return home.

"She come in and, uh . . . she went . . . went to the back bedroom and I was in the living room. I come out of the living room, she was coming back down this way like she didn't see me. She was going for her bathroom. And then . . . then she seen the window was broken, she . . . she was like running toward the front of the house. So I accosted her."

He took her into the bedroom, the .25-caliber automatic snug in his hand. It was the same gun that he'd used to assault Leslie the second time.

Just like he'd done with Leslie, he forced the woman to disrobe.

"Do you recall what she may have been wearing?" Smith asked.

Krajcir drew a blank.

"Um . . ."

"What month of the year it was?" Smith coerced.

"Maybe February, March, maybe. Somewhere in there. I'm not sure. I'm not sure about the date." But he correctly remembered that it had been 1982.

"Yeah . . . uh . . . I made her . . . asked her to disrobe. She was scared and she went along with the program. And again, I had her perform oral sex."

He didn't think he'd had intercourse with her.

"Let's jump back a minute. How did you get inside the residence again?" Smith said.

"Through the bathroom window."

"Was it open? Did you have to break it?"

Krajcir admitted to breaking the glass. He remembered having to brush glass fragments away.

"I might have knocked something off the shelf there.

250

If there . . . there was something on there, but I really [don't] remember it."

He said he could have been wearing gloves that night, brown woven ones, but he wasn't sure.

"And that particular night, you had only been to that residence one time before?" Smith asked.

"Yes."

"Looked through the window? After you saw her return home, you followed her home from the Kroger store. Is that correct?"

"Yes . . . I remember when I was at the Kroger store, I would get a better look at her."

He might have even gone in and purchased some of the rawhide strings to tie up the victim, about a week before her death. He remembered the payment book that Margie Call carried with her when he saw her at the store.

A week later, he returned, intending to sexually assault the woman he'd seen at the store. The detectives returned to their line of questioning.

"I think the lights were on in the house," Krajcir said.

He hadn't rifled through anything while he waited, but he peeped out toward the carport through the blinds.

It was his first time inside the residence. When the woman came in, and he stopped her from running, he took her into the bathroom, but ended up moving back to the bedroom. The blown-out window made the little bathroom too chilly.

"The window was broken and there was cold air coming in. I remember that. Uh . . . then all I did was took her back in the bedroom. I think I tied her up."

"Do you recall what with?"

"I think I had a couple of shoestrings or . . . my . . . I'm not sure," Krajcir said. He remembered killing her, even the strangulation, but he didn't quite remember how he'd done it. He couldn't recall whether he'd used his bare hands, or a handkerchief, maybe the legendary blue bandanna itself.

He didn't remember gagging her either.

"Was she cooperative?" Smith asked.

"Yes."

"Did you have to strike her?"

"No."

"Do you recall if the bed was made or unmade?"

"It was made."

"Were there any pillows removed from the bed?"

"I . . . I can't recall. I don't think so. I don't remember taking any pillows or anything."

"You said you tied her up with the ligatures. Is that the way you left her?" Smith asked.

Krajcir didn't really remember doing anything after he tied her up.

"I just cut out of there real quick."

One significant detail about this particular murder was definitely needed here. In order for the confession to be believable, Krajcir had to tell them about the severed nipple.

"Do you recall using the restroom afterward?" Smith prompted him.

Krajcir said no.

"Do you recall trying to flush anything down [the toilet]?"

"No."

"Were there any injuries to her body?" Smith asked.

"Um . . . not that I'm aware of, no."

"Like, would you have bitten her anywhere? That you recall?" Smith asked the question as though it could easily have slipped someone's mind—having taken a bite out of a body part.

"Okay." Krajcir knew where this was headed now. "I was gonna take a . . . a souvenir if I'm not mistaken. And I . . . I . . . cut one of her nipples."

"How did you do that?" Smith asked.

"With a knife," he said.

Smith asked if he recalled on which side of her chest it had been, and Krajcir answered he believed it was the left. He wasn't sure.

"Did you, in fact, take it with you?"

"No, I think I might have flushed it."

Krajcir remembered having taken some cash from inside the house—he thought it came from church envelopes or something similar. Rarely had he left the scene of any of his crimes totally empty-handed.

"I think I emptied those. I'm not sure if she had any money in her purse or not. I can't remember that."

Smith asked if he cut the ligatures, but Krajcir didn't recall that either.

"Why did you decide to kill her?" There it was again, that question he just couldn't answer.

"I'd say at the time I . . . I had never planned to kill any of them, but they just . . . I don't know why, some of them I . . . I killed. And then some of them, I didn't."

It was a question that plagued the victims even more

than it perplexed Krajcir. Why did some survive the attacks?

He couldn't say what the trigger had been that time, with Margie Call.

"Did she do anything to make you mad?" Smith asked.

"No."

"She was cooperative throughout?"

"Yes."

"Do you remember anything she may have said to you? At any point?"

Krajcir thought he remembered Margie saying something about her teeth, but again, he couldn't really be certain.

"I think I did smoke [a cigarette] inside the residence," he said.

"Do you know what you may have done with your . . . with your butt when you disposed of it?"

"No . . . I'm not too sure. I might've flushed it."

"Okay. Have you ever smoked Benson and Hedges cigarettes?" Smith asked.

"No." Krajcir answered truthfully. He generally smoked Marlboro Lights.

"Did you happen to cut yourself that night or tear any piece of clothing that could have been left outside?"

"I could have leaving. I don't remember that. I know crawling through all that glass I might have left something there."

He never knew her name, and he generally didn't ask the names of his victims.

"Did she remove all of her clothing?" Smith asked.

"Yeah, I think so," Krajcir said, referring to one of the details he seemed fairly quick to grab from his memory. He nearly always remembered the clothing.

"During the sex act, was there any type of clothing that you recall that she may have been wearing? Maybe on your direction?"

He didn't remember the boots Margie Call had on her feet that night. After seeing the picture of the woman lying on the bed, he guessed she did keep them on during the assault.

"Can you think of anything else concerning this incident that you want to tell us about?" Smith asked.

"To know that I was there? You mean like a detail?"

"I'm sorry?" Smith questioned.

"You mean like a detail?" Krajcir asked.

"Yeah, anything you can recall. Your own recollection."

Krajcir paused. "Uh . . . the basement door . . . was locked. I remember that. Uh . . . I think she had a . . . part of the front of the house on the front side blocked. The heating was off, but the doors were unlocked."

He'd left the residence that night by the carport entrance.

"Do you recall, altogether, how long you were in the residence that night?" Smith asked.

"Probably from when I went in initially till I left . . . maybe an hour. Hour and five minutes. Usually when . . . when the woman would come home, I mean it would be real quick."

He tried to make it quick.

"And I'd be gone," he finished.

A few more questions about whether he'd tried to flush the ligature pieces down the toilet, and the puzzling rose on the bed, and they moved on to talking about the murder of Mildred Wallace.

"Again, it was the same MO. I followed her home from Kroger's."

"How long before this particular night are we talking about? You followed her home?" Smith asked.

It had been the same night he'd spotted her, Krajcir explained.

"That's the first time you ever saw this lady?"

"Yes. I think it was a Sunday night. I was real frantic. Usually on a Sunday night I would never go out."

"How long had you been in town when you saw her that night?"

He thought it was probably after eight at night.

"And I parked right there. Maybe a block away. Went down the road. I was looking in the bathroom window. She'd . . . it was after she'd pulled in and went into the house. And I was . . . I was looking in the window, she put her coat back on. And left."

Smith murmured in the affirmative, and Krajcir continued.

She'd gone somewhere, and then he'd seized the opportunity to enter the house.

"I smashed her window. And, uh . . . I remember I cut myself right here somewhere. My left hand was a little cut."

It only bled a little bit, and he found a bandage for the cut in her bathroom.

"It was almost like she went out to get a newspaper or

something. I'm not exactly sure. Anyway, I was waiting in the . . . a . . . room down at the end of the hall. And she went into the bedroom. Started taking her clothes off. Or took the coat off. And then I came down the hallway and accosted her in the bedroom. I made her take her clothes off. I had a . . . a gun and I threatened her with the gun."

He'd gotten that pistol from a burglary he'd committed in Marion.

Echols made the connection immediately to one of the first cases they'd asked Krajcir about. He was talking about one of the Marion sexual assaults he'd emphatically denied knowing anything about earlier. It was all coming out in the wash now, it seemed.

"She didn't give me the impression that she was that old. I mean she was a younger-looking woman."

He admitted to the forcible rape. He didn't recall having tied her up at that point, but couldn't say with absolute certainty.

"If you would have tied her up, what would you have used?" Smith asked.

"Probably some of all the same thing, I guess."

He remembered looking around her house while he waited.

"I looked for money. Any valuables. Went back in the room. I walked real softly in there. And then shot her one time and . . . left."

He had aimed for her head, he believed. She had been lying facedown on the bed, he thought, when he fired.

Smith asked for details again, anything Krajcir could retrieve from his memory.

"I remember she asked me if . . . I was the guy who

killed a woman across the street, one that we were just talking about."

He also knew she had kept something in her kitchen to block the door.

"I . . . I may have cut . . . cut the telephone line, but I don't . . ."

"Do you specifically remember that?" Smith wanted to be sure Krajcir wasn't just responding to prompts.

"No. I had [done this] in other incidents."

He did remember putting a towel in the broken window this time, not wanting the breeze blowing in to make Mildred run like Margie Call had done.

"Did she get a good look at your face?" Smith asked.

"I don't think so, 'cause I had a bandanna on."

Smith asked what his reason for shooting her had been—again, the unanswerable question.

"There wasn't any reason. I wasn't . . . knowing this was in my head." She hadn't fought him. "She went along with the program." He continued trying to explain where he'd been coming from, but he really had no idea. "I didn't have reason hardly to kill any of these women."

"Just the point you didn't want . . . you didn't want to leave any witnesses?" Smith asked. That maybe had been how it had started. "That's the only reason you can think of?"

"I think there might have been more to it . . . you know I thought about why do I . . . why do I sometimes I kill them and sometimes I don't, you know? And a lot . . . of women I killed resembled my mother. You know . . . agewise and . . . uh . . . body build and . . ."

Margie Call and Mildred Wallace had both resembled

his mother slightly, he said. He couldn't help wondering aloud if that had been lingering somewhere in the back of his mind all along.

"I think that was in there somewhere."

"Can you describe your mother?" Smith asked. Krajcir had always talked about his family in vague terms, during his previous interviews.

He'd been incarcerated when she passed away. He'd only seen her once or twice while he was in prison, and by that time her health had seriously deteriorated. She suffered from both diabetes and congestive heart failure.

"When she was younger, she was a real attractive woman," he said, though she hadn't aged as well as she could have, due to her health problems.

"I had this fetish for women with nice-looking butts," he confessed.

He thought that the fetish may have stemmed from an experience he had as a child, when he'd walked in on his mother dressing.

"And I remembered she hollered and screamed at me. And, uh . . . I think I was six or seven years old. And I remember, uh . . . it set off kind of weird things to me and I was embarrassed and got flushed and . . . and it got me really encrusted in my mind," he explained.

They wrapped up the interview with a discussion of a couple of details, such as where he'd tossed that pistol after using it to shoot Mildred Wallace in the head. He remembered throwing it toward some railroad tracks he'd found off a little turnaround spot on Route 3 as he headed home to Carbondale.

A week later, Swingle found probable cause to charge

Timothy Krajcir with five of Cape Girardeau's unsolved murders, and three sexual assaults by way of forcible rapes. Two of the sexual assaults had been those committed against Margie Call and Mildred Wallace. Count number three was the second time Krajcir had raped Leslie. (Because she hadn't reported the first assault to the police, the statute of limitations had long since run its course.) All eight charges carried potential life sentences.

The town of Cape Girardeau buzzed with the news that the murders had been solved for about three weeks before a judge even signed his name to an arrest warrant formally charging Krajcir. Conspiratorial whispers echoed in coffee shops, and family members of victims shared information with members of the local media. So did police, though the agreement was to keep the story under wraps until charges were official. Everyone had heard at least a little—that they were making an arrest, that the perpetrator was an outsider, and that he was already in prison for another crime.

On December 10, the city called a news conference at a local convention center to announce the charges against Krajcir. It was a media blitz. TV and print media from St. Louis to the Associated Press turned out for it. The local KFVS12 station set up a live feed. Even the *New York Times* sent a stringer to cover the event.

A panel of investigators and others associated with the case stood by a long table in the front of the room. Swingle was standing front and center at a podium. Jay Knudson, mayor of Cape Girardeau, was there, along with Detective Jimmy Smith, Lieutenant Detective Paul

Echols, Cape Girardeau police chief Carl Kinnison, and a DNA analyst who'd worked on matching the evidence with Timothy Krajcir.

Members of the vast Call family sat together in the folding chairs designated for the audience. Only a single niece remained to represent the Wallace clan. Sheila Cole's family, as well as Parsh relatives, chose not to attend the news conference, fearing it would be too upsetting.

"For the family members of the victims of these crimes, there can never really be justice," Kinnison told the crowd of about a hundred citizens, former officers, and relatives. At this point, maybe justice was too much to hope for; perhaps closure was enough.

Mildred Wallace's niece, Teresa Haubold, said that the decision to accept Krajcir's confession or seek the death penalty had been one of the easiest choices her family had ever had to make. They wanted closure for all of the families this man had hurt, not just their own.

Teresa had gone to high school with both Brenda Parsh and her sister, Karen, and had grown up in the same neighborhood. She knew the way that the police officers who worked those cases had kept the victims' memory alive all these years, and she couldn't express enough gratitude for their diligence.

Don Call, Margie's son, said that discovering the identity of his mother's killer didn't erase all of the guilt he felt, and he knew his brother had felt, for living in other cities when she was murdered. It only solved part of the problem; it couldn't take away what happened, he said.

Vicki Abernathy was the only attendee who was there

specifically because of Mary and Brenda Parsh. She and Brenda had been friends in high school, and the former stewardess still felt a strong connection with her. She clutched a photograph of herself and Brenda at the Watermelon Queen beauty contest late in the 1960s; at the time, Brenda had been the retiring queen.

Prosecutor Morley Swingle explained that Timothy Krajcir had at this point confessed to a total of nine murders, including one he'd pleaded guilty to that morning in Illinois, that of Deborah Sheppard. A Jackson County judge in Illinois had only hours earlier accepted Krajcir's guilty plea in that killing. Krajcir received a forty-year sentence for the murder. Swingle presented a brief case history of the five Cape Girardeau murders, and explained that Detective Smith had been working them for several months.

He ran through the basics of what gave authorities probable cause to charge Timothy Krajcir with the string of homicides. He understood that since so much time had passed, the citizens of the town might need convincing that they had the right guy.

A $10 million bond was placed on Krajcir's head. Such a number was all but unheard of in Cape Girardeau. A member of the media asked Swingle whether or not it was fair to call Krajcir a serial killer at this point. Swingle replied that the legal definition of a serial killer is someone who kills more than three times in succession, and invited the crowd to "do the math" on their own.

Chapter 11

Loose Ends

On January 3, 2008, Detectives Paul Echols and Jimmy Smith again sat in an interview room with now alleged serial killer Timothy Wayne Krajcir. This would be a cleanup interview, one meant to tie up any loose ends in the investigation, and to learn more about the man behind the crimes. This time they were at Tamms Correctional Center in Tamms, Illinois, not far from Carbondale.

Legally and procedurally, all of the chips had fallen into place. Timothy Krajcir faced a slew of murder and forcible rape charges across the area of the Midwest known as the Heartland. McCracken County, in Kentucky, was still discussing whether or not to file charges against him for the murder of Joyce Tharp, the pretty young black woman found discarded in an alley in the Paducah neighborhood of Forest Hill. Since Tharp had been killed in Carbondale and her body driven across state lines, technically, the murder charges needed to come from Jackson County, Illinois, where the killing occurred.

Similar circumstances existed in Cape Girardeau County and Alexander County, Illinois, the area where Sheila Cole had been murdered. Kidnapping a victim from one state and killing her in another had created legal problems when it came to choosing which jurisdiction should file the charges. For a brief time, the Alexander County state's attorney considered the possibility of filing the murder charge in his own jurisdiction. The sexual assault had occurred in Carbondale, throwing yet another jurisdiction into the mix. But Mike Weipsic, state's attorney in Carbondale, Jackson County, had made it clear there would be no more charges against Timothy Krajcir coming from his office.

Although the murder of Sheila Cole hadn't occurred in Morley Swingle's county, the prosecutor's grounds for charging Krajcir were based on the premise that one element of the crime had occurred in his jurisdiction. Since the crime had been planned and initiated in Cape Girardeau, he could charge Krajcir with the murder.

The purpose of that January interview with Krajcir was to get further details out of him, and to cast a wider net for information that could lead to quickly wrapping up any other unsolved cases of the kind they now knew he'd committed.

The detectives began talking about Krajcir's travels

between Illinois and Pennsylvania, keeping the tone of the interview more conversational, and less businesslike, than the earlier ones.

Krajcir talked about a dog he'd had, a little lab named Smokey.

Echols remembered seeing some pictures of Krajcir and the dog at a lake. Kracjir had given Echols permission to glance through the pages of a scrapbook he'd kept, and the detective had done so in the interest of learning more about the puzzling killer.

"What lake was that? Was that Crab Orchard?" Echols asked.

"No, it was . . . on Campus Lake." Krajcir said, referring to Southern Illinois University.

"Oh, Campus Lake. On Campus Lake?"

"Uh-huh," Krajcir replied.

"Okay. And since . . . you bring it up on campus, was there ever anything you did on campus?"

Krajcir said, no, there hadn't been.

"So there was no sexual assaults? Nothing like that?"

Again, Krajcir said no.

They got around to clearing up some details of the Sheila Cole homicide.

"Now, when you took her into that trailer, there in Carbondale, do you remember performing oral sex on her?" Echols asked. "And the reason that I ask that is, the crime lab tells me that the DNA that they're getting might be . . . [more] consistent with . . . your saliva than it would be [with] your semen."

"I don't think so," Krajcir said.

"Do you remember having vaginal sex with her at all?" Echols was trying to understand how Krajcir's DNA had gotten on Sheila Cole's jeans.

"I don't know unless her clothes were lying close to the bed and she spit some of it out," Krajcir said.

"So it was on the bed where this took place?" Echols asked.

"Yeah, it was in the little . . . it's a real little tiny room."

"That was in the trailer?"

"Yeah."

"I've not been in that trailer, actually, [but] the trailer is still there . . . it had . . . a bedroom on one end and one in the middle?" Echols slowly worked out the information in his head.

"Yeah."

"How was it set up?"

"Pretty much like that."

"So you had the bedroom in the middle?"

Krajcir murmured affirmatively.

"And so you took Sheila Cole into that bedroom?"

"Yeah."

"And do you remember step-by-step how that took place? . . . She still had clothes on, I'm sure, when you brought her in," Echols reasoned.

"Uh-huh," Krajcir said again in a murmur.

"And she took her clothes off?"

"She took her clothes off right there in the bedroom there. I don't know if she laid them to the side or . . . dropped them or . . . I . . ." his voice trailed off.

"It's been thirty years, but . . ." Echols followed some

other lines of inquiry, then changed subjects. "In regard to Paducah and the black girl that was abducted from Paducah. Just to run through a couple of things. You told a detective . . . or Assistant Chief Danny Carroll when we interviewed [you] last time here, that when you went into her bedroom she had some type of a . . . sleeping mask on."

That was a detail the family couldn't corroborate. Echols asked if Krajcir was certain about the mask.

"Yeah, I was pretty sure of that," he said. "A little mask over her eyes."

He remembered walking into her bedroom and looking at her just as she was beginning to wake up. She still had it over her eyes. He kept it on her because it offered him another layer of protection.

His memory seemed pretty sharp about that fact, so Echols dropped it. He moved on to the discussion of Ida White, the little old lady Krajcir said he'd stabbed in Mount Vernon.

"That's right across the street from the post office," Krajcir said, looking at the photo.

"Was it an apartment or a house?" Echols asked.

"Well, I think it was a house, which they were . . . they were split into apartments," Krajcir replied. "This woman had an apartment on the lower left-hand side of the building."

Echols confirmed that the victim had also been a white woman.

"I remember seeing somewhere that they arrested someone for that. And then, uh . . . turned them loose," Krajcir said.

This bit of information was indeed new.

"Oh, so you think they arrested somebody?" Echols asked.

"Yeah, I remember seeing that somewhere. Reading it or seeing it somewhere. They arrested somebody . . . I think it was a black guy, too. I'm not a hundred percent on that. I remember they arrested somebody for that."

"And you think they turned him loose, or you're not sure?" Echols asked.

"I'm not positive, but I think he got turned loose."

"So somebody could be in prison for that?" Echols was concerned, and reasonably so.

"Possibility," Krajcir said.

"And that was the stabbing, the one that involved the stabbing?"

"Yes."

"Okay. You said that . . . you crawled through a basement window."

"No."

It had been an apartment window, but it was the bathroom window on the left side, and getting inside hadn't been that easy.

"It wasn't a basement?" Echols asked.

"Well, I think it was the basement of the house, but I think it was a basement apartment," Krajcir said, gesturing with his arm to show them exactly where the window had been in relation to the ground and his body.

"Yeah. Oh, okay. And you accosted her in the bathroom?"

"Yeah, I was hiding in the shower when she walked in."

"Were you there very long? I mean, was she at home when you broke in?" Echols asked.

Krajcir answered that yes, she had been.

"Okay. And then so . . . you were just hiding in there. Did she hear a noise and come in or did she just . . ." Echols trailed off.

"I think she was just getting ready for bed."

Echols asked where the shower curtain had been, whether it had concealed his menacing presence or not.

Krajcir had been behind it, he explained, but it was pulled back, so she couldn't see around it until she fully entered the little bathroom.

"Okay, so you had [gone] into that and then she came in. You crawled through the window and went into that shower and kind of hid?" Echols asked Krajcir to just run through how it had gone down from that moment.

"She came in. Come in the bathroom. Tried to go to the bathroom or something. And as soon as she sat down, I accosted her. And, uh . . . [she] kept on screaming. Trying to scream and I had . . . my hand over her mouth, trying to stop her from screaming."

"You were standing behind her?" Echols asked.

It had been more like he stood *over* her while she screamed, Krajcir explained. "And that went on a couple of minutes like that. Just screaming, screaming. Wouldn't stop screaming." It had gone on for a couple of minutes. "She was a pretty feisty old gal. And, uh . . . that's when, uh . . . when I got the knife out. Tell her to please stop . . . stop . . . stop. I'm not gonna hurt you. Stop. I'm not gonna hurt you. Stop. She just kept on screaming. And, uh . . . I stabbed her. A couple of times."

"Where did you stab her at?" Echols inquired.

"I think it was in around her stomach area. Or in the side."

"Was she still sitting when you did that?"

At that point, she may have dropped to the floor, Krajcir thought.

"I think I only stabbed like maybe two, maybe three times," he said.

She stopped screaming then, and went totally quiet. That was when he'd taken off.

"Back out the same window you came in?" Echols asked.

Krajcir said yes, that's how he'd gotten back out. He didn't quite remember how he knew someone had been arrested for that crime. He thought he had either heard it around town or seen it somewhere, but didn't know for sure.

"And you said as far as you know, she lived?" Echols asked, wondering aloud if there was any way that fact could be verified. They still hadn't found the police report, assuming the woman had called the police. She must have sought medical treatment.

"I mean this . . . if you're hearing it, then everybody knew about it. The police knew about it. But they've recently moved their records, so they're having a difficult time finding the report."

Echols had a couple of reasons for wanting to track down these police reports. First of all, if a man was in prison for something that Krajcir did, he shouldn't be there. Second, it only seemed right that the victim, if she was still alive, be told what had happened so she could have some real closure.

"I don't imagine she's still alive," Krajcir said.

He hadn't known her real age, but even then, she didn't seem like she was in the best of health.

Echols moved on to the next set of questions he had for Krajcir.

He asked about the sexual assaults he'd committed in Illinois, in Marion and Johnston City, interested to know if Krajcir recalled when they had been.

"I know I had the Plymouth, so it had to be . . . '82 or late '81," Krajcir said.

"Okay. Do you remember what time of the year?"

"Yeah, it was warm. It was late summer, or . . . or summer. Because I remember I only had the T-shirt on."

The first sexual assault in Marion had been near Ida White's house, by the post office, near where the stabbing occurred.

"Anything else about that case you remember? Anything else about the inside of it? Anything you remember about the lady? The hair color? Anything . . ." Echols said.

"I remember when I opened the window, I took some stuff that was on the shelf there. A . . . window ledge and I threw it out. So I could crawl in," Krajcir explained. Other than that, there wasn't much he could recall.

"Okay. Through the last several months, as you can guess, there [were] several interviews done with some of your former cell mates. That's no mystery to you. I know that you're aware of that. You had told one of your cell

mates that there was a body in Pennsylvania, that someday you would give up a body in Pennsylvania. I'm not
sure if it was in Pennsylvania."

Krajcir had wanted to get back there someday, and
wanted to tell the police about the case in South Temple.
He'd called it a body, but all he meant was another unsolved homicide.

"So that's the only body that there was?" Echols wanted
to be certain.

"Yeah."

"And that's the one in Pennsylvania? There's no bodies anywhere else?"

Krajcir didn't think so. Dumping the bodies of his
victims just hadn't been his routine. He almost always
assaulted, killed, and left them in their own beds.

"I mean, when you say you don't think so, that automatically makes me wonder if there . . . I mean, you
know you've gone this far, if there was anything else.
Now's the time to do it," Echols told him.

"No . . . there's nothing else. We got it all."

"Nothing came to mind from Cape? Like . . . oh, a
house burglary or anything that you happen to [have]
thought of since?

Echols didn't mention that feelers had already been
put out in every community Krajcir had preyed anywhere
near, for any unsolved cases that suggested Krajcir's
MO.

They'd already located the robbery of Elza and Eunice Seabaugh, Smith told him.

"The woman is still alive. She's eighty-eight years
old," Smith informed him. "She's not living in Cape any-

more, but she's still alive. And I have a copy of the report. They described you rather well." The report also noted that he'd been wearing "a blue shirt, blue jeans, and a dark-colored handkerchief or bandanna over the lower part of his face." Krajcir agreed that that had been him.

"Sounds like the old guy was pretty feisty," Echols said.

"Yeah, he was. He was."

"How did you happen to locate that house? Do you remember?"

"Just cruising. You know, walking around a neighborhood looking for victims," Krajcir said. He'd pretty much been strolling from block to block on foot. He stopped when he saw the couple inside their home.

Echols cut in quickly.

"Let me ask another question . . . you know you . . . apparently said to us and some of the inmates who you'd talked to through the years, that you didn't hunt in your own backyard. You didn't want to do crimes around Carbondale. But isn't it kind of ironic [that] that's the one that got you caught?" Echols observed.

"Yeah. Went against my own rule. Right." The irony did not appear to be lost on Krajcir.

"And . . . do you remember why you did that?" Echols asked.

"Well, see it's like I said, rationality goes out the window. You get the need and the urge and you gotta do something," Krajcir said.

"And so in regard to Deborah Sheppard's case, you had been over in that area looking in windows before . . ." Echols began. "And you'd [gone] back . . . I mean . . . had you seen her in there . . . undressing before or is it . . ."

Krajcir admitted to having spied on Deborah Sheppard once before. He thought she was fully dressed, but she looked very attractive, and it piqued his interest.

"Again it was the dark area around there," Krajcir said. He'd thought the fact that there were no streetlamps nearby would keep him fairly well protected.

"So you went against your own rule and it caught up with you," Echols said again.

The detectives rapidly switched topics.

"This is not much of a map, but it's a map of the McClure area. You told us at one point the gun that was used in the Wallace case, I think you took it from a home in Marion. Is that right?" Smith showed him the map. "And you said you threw it . . . out of your car on the way back."

He asked if this had occurred on a side road.

"I think it was a side road that went back," Krajcir said.

"Be off to the right as you're going toward Carbondale?" Smith asked.

"Yeah. Yeah. Yeah. There's a . . . railroad tracks."

"Crossed over the railroad tracks?" Smith asked.

Krajcir said he'd stopped just before.

"There's no landmarks that you remember?" Echols said.

"I think there was a road going this way. And railroad tracks running like here. Farm. Woods over here." That part of southern Illinois was almost entirely wooded farmland. Krajcir could have been talking about any number of spots on Route 3.

"You just gave it a toss out in the woods?" Smith asked.

"Yeah. I came like right over here. And swish . . ." Krajcir gestured.

He'd thrown it straight across the track, and it landed somewhere off in the woods.

"Was it just the gun, or did you throw something else along with it?" Smith asked.

Krajcir said he'd only gotten rid of the gun at that time.

The detectives then asked about a few other unsolved homicides from the area, but none rang a bell with Krajcir. Echols and Smith's phones had been ringing off the hook with calls from departments wondering if Krajcir had lived anywhere in their vicinities, or had traveled through them, wondering if there could be a connection between him and their backlog of unsolved cases.

"So . . . we promise these guys that we would ask, because . . . you're being truthful and that's all they can ask."

"Now, I know you disclosed some things that we didn't have any idea about," Smith said. "And I understand that you were trying to be as helpful as you could, but I just didn't want anything to throw a monkey wrench into the agreement you made with the prosecutor, you know, that you would disclose everything."

"And we also know that there's so much," Echols added, and "you've done remarkably well to keep it from getting confused, but also know that there . . . along the way there's been a couple of things that you'd forgotten, that you'd helped us line out. So, that's why we wanted to come back one last time. To see if there was anything else that you'd thought of."

"How do you feel personally after all of this . . . after disclos[ing] all of this? How do you feel? About yourself?" Smith asked. It seemed like a loaded question, especially considering the man he was asking.

"Is it a relief?" Echols wondered aloud.

"I don't know if you would call it a relief," Krajcir answered. "[I've been] sort of . . . numb for a while . . . and like I say, when I was looking at some of that stuff, and I was thinking God, how could I do that? You know, and . . . I don't know."

"If you had to do it all over again, would you . . . disclose everything that you've done so far, like you did? Would you do anything different?" Echols asked.

"Well, I think I was gonna disclose, but like I said, I was gonna wait till my health started to fail." Krajcir insisted he really would have disclosed his misdeeds then.

"I guess you can't answer that question until a few years down the line when you finally see where you settle out," Echols said.

Krajcir agreed.

"Where you're gonna land," Echols added.

"But if this . . . you know . . . if this helps the families and stuff . . ." Krajcir said.

Echols assured him it helped the families. Of that there could be no doubt in anyone's mind.

"It's been a great relief for a lot of people," Smith said. "It has. I mean . . . there's been enough time that has elapsed from your crime[s] till now that . . . there's a lot of emotions involved for sure, but I think the . . . the emotion of hatred isn't there, as strong as it would be. It's more of a . . . relief. Knowing that they finally have closure. The young lady who we talked about [during] the snowstorm, the young lady that you raped in February of '79? . . . It was very, very much a relief to her that she can finally, now, put this behind her."

"You're a smart guy and you do understand how this would be . . . it's a horrible thing," Echols added. "That part's done, though. You can't do anything about what's already happened. The only part you can deal with now is the aftereffects . . . even though it's been so many years . . . It has allowed [the families] to finally take a breath and a sigh of relief and know that the person who is responsible is being punished, and I can move on now with my life. And I don't have to look over my shoulder wondering and . . . and being suspicious of people who don't deserve to be . . . treated that way, because, just because they didn't know. And now they do know. So I think that makes sense to you."

Smith remembered something. When Krajcir had made the perp walk to the Jackson County Courthouse for the hearing in which he pleaded guilty for the Sheppard killing, a tall, gray-haired gentleman had held the door of the courthouse for him.

"The person who held the door open for you was Margie Call's son," Smith informed him.

"Yeah, he gave me a couple of good looks. I remember him," Krajcir admitted.

The charges against Krajcir had given the man a lot of relief, and closure, Echols said.

"I mean he . . . was very relieved to know finally what the story was. And what happened to his mother. I mean it's not like this was gonna be so traumatic to him. He already knew pretty much what happened. He just didn't know who did it. And so now he does."

The conversation moved on to Krajcir's childhood and youth, as well as his short-lived marriage.

"Did you say at one time you had a daughter?" Smith asked.

Krajcir said that yes, he did. His daughter, Charlotte, had been born in early summer 1963.

"Ever hear from her?" Smith asked.

"No . . . I think [her mother] probably told her I was killed in a car wreck or something. I don't . . . I don't know."

Then Krajcir shared with the two detectives a strange and almost uncanny experience he'd had concerning his daughter. He'd been at the Pennsylvania State Correctional Institution at Graterford.

"Anyway, I was thinking of getting in this program where you teach other guys how to get their GED, you know. So do math for them. Help them, you know, one of those kind of programs. And this gal showed a movie about learning to help people, right. And the movie was made in Syracuse University. This girl walks right up to the camera. She's got a name tag on, right. And it said Charlotte."

The girl had been tall, for a female, with dark hair. She'd borne an eerily close resemblance to an aunt of Krajcir's.

"I just wondered. I said God, could that possibly be my daughter, you know? I checked the age and everything. The age had been right. I mean, it's a weird experience."

He talked about living on a naval base before getting married.

"So when you actually got in trouble," Echols noted, "based upon the old reports that I read, there were more than two sexual assaults, but that's what you got charged with."

There had only been two, Krajcir acknowledged, unless you counted the one he'd been about to commit the night he'd been caught.

He'd already had his clothes off, and crept into a basement, waiting.

"You had looked in windows even back in Pennsylvania, but you had never acted out," Echols said.

There had been no rapes prior to him joining the navy, Krajcir confirmed.

"Okay, so you get caught and so then you get sent to prison," Echols began.

Krajcir had been sent to Menard Psychiatric center for five years. The nuthouse, he called it.

"That's the worst thing that ever happened to me," he said.

He talked briefly about playing on the basketball team in prison.

"I saw your newspaper clippings. You were pretty good," Echols said.

He'd played on the prison baseball team as well, until he got a transfer to Vienna, a minimum security prison, in 1972. The prison also sent inmates to umpire baseball games all over the area, giving Krajcir the opportunity to travel, but for the most part, he didn't take advantage of this. Basketball kept him busy, and so did the EMT classes he was taking. When he got out of prison, Krajcir began working for an ambulance service based out of a hospital. The guys used to cover for one another, whenever one of them had a girlfriend, and they had a whole system worked out. They used the ambulance siren as a warning signal so the man who was out would be alerted that their supervisor was either nearby or on his way back soon.

At the time, Krajcir had been seeing an LPN who worked at the same hospital as he did.

"The women went nuts over the convicts. I mean you wouldn't believe it. I mean, from the ugliest guy to the handsomest guy. Married women, younger women, it was unreal," Krajcir said.

"So there was a lot of sex going on?" Echols asked.

"Oh, man, they had to chase them away." Krajcir laughed.

"So it goes to show none of this was really for sex, because you never had any problems there," Echols put in.

"I still had a little bit of problems," Krajcir corrected.

He'd had some problems attracting women, he said.

"It was all about power. Control. It was never . . . sex was not the prime ingredient there. Most serious rapists, it's just almost the same way. It's power and control. It's not so much the actual sexual thing. I mean instant gratification is there, but it's so quick it just . . . it doesn't, you know, take care of the need. So . . . like a week later . . . you can be out doing the same thing again. The same kind of need." Krajcir struggled to explain.

Echols brought him back around to the reason for the interview, and referenced Virginia Witte, the woman from Marion he'd killed. Krajcir admitted that he must have been feeling desperate to have committed a murder in broad daylight. That was the only time he'd ever killed someone during the daytime.

He'd very nearly gotten caught, too, though he had only recently been made aware of this. His parole officer had called the Williamson County Major Case Squad and told them that the composite sketch from a witness resembled Krajcir. They checked his car out when they learned that he'd been off duty that day and had no alibi, but they never interviewed him in connection with the murder.

It was shortly after killing the Witte woman that Krajcir got caught with the adolescent girl in Carbondale, and it was back to Menard.

"All the crazy people were gone by then. And they still didn't have no program there. But all the crazy people were gone and it was a lot different than it had been the first time," he said.

He'd gone back to counseling in prison, but the therapy didn't work, because he hadn't been committed to it. He'd gone along with it, gone through the motions, and it convinced the counselors.

"It's easy to slide through a system that's so over-crowded," he said.

Toward the end of the interview, Smith asked a question about the Parsh homicide.

"You said the Parshes were the first time you really stepped over the line. How did you feel within yourself after that happened? Say the next few days or so?"

"Honest with you. I didn't think about it at all," Krajcir

said bluntly. He had gone to a friend's wedding the next day, and he didn't think that it crossed his mind once that he'd killed a mother and daughter the day before.

"It was just about like it was as callous as it sounds. It's the truth. That part of me just wasn't there," he explained. He'd only ever cared about people he knew. Those people he knew, he could never do anything to hurt. He only preyed on strangers.

Chapter 12

Convicted

The months leading up to Krajcir's court appearance in Cape Girardeau seemed to drag, for him as well as for the families of his many victims. Transferring an inmate from state to state doesn't necessarily go smoothly, and there were a lot of snags along the way. When Krajcir was first charged with the eight felonies, Swingle's intention was for the speediest extradition possible under the circumstances.

Immediately after the charges were final, Missouri governor Matt Blunt signed an order of extradition requesting Krajcir's transfer to the Cape Girardeau County Jail, where he would await trial for his crimes. Sheriff's deputies began implementing plans to transport the man from the supermax correctional facility in Tamms, Illinois, where he was serving a forty-year sentence for the

Sheppard killing, to the jail in Jackson, Missouri. Jackson, a small town just north of Cape Girardeau, served as the county seat, and housed the jail and courthouse.

Cape Girardeau County sheriff John Jordan intended to accompany the officers who were bringing Krajcir back over the river. He'd never seen a serial killer, and he wanted the opportunity to speak with the man whose actions had haunted Cape Girardeau for so many years.

Governor Blunt was prepared for the extradition process to take up to thirty days, but officials expedited the request as much as possible. Swingle's investigator personally drove across the state to Jefferson City to hand-deliver the twenty-four-page document to the governor's office.

The crimes Krajcir had committed elsewhere slowed things down a bit. Chuck Garnati, the Williamson County, Illinois, state's attorney, announced after he charged Krajcir with killing Virginia Lee Witte that he wanted the inmate to stay in Illinois until the case was resolved.

Krajcir's initial court date in Missouri, where he would hear the formal charges the state had levied against him, was supposed to occur on December 27, 2007, but the Illinois state's attorney filed charges in the Witte murder late Christmas Eve. Blunt expressed his frustration at the delay in the process, but he and Swingle had no choice but to agree to let Williamson County settle their murder charges first. Williamson County would get first crack at Timothy Krajcir.

Illinois prison officials had a lot to do with the decision. Everyone was aware that Krajcir, though in his sixties and in failing health, was still a dangerous man. He'd attempted to escape from prison once, and he was currently housed in a supermax facility. The less he had to be shuffled back and forth across state lines, the better for public safety and taxpayer expense, it seemed.

While Krajcir sat in the Illinois prison awaiting his day in court, he was hit with more murder charges. A grand jury in Paducah, Kentucky, indicted him in the kidnapping and murder of Joyce Tharp.

Less than a week later, Krajcir set foot in a courtroom for the first time in over twenty years. The small courtroom allowed him to be slipped in through an internal entrance, so corrections officers could avoid flashbulbs and potential assassination attempts—Krajcir had begun to receive death threats as soon as the charges were filed. He was ushered in through the courthouse's sally port, which meant that he didn't have to leave the car that was transporting him till he was nearly in the courtroom.

As the first order of business, Chuck Garnati waived the death penalty, as Swingle had done. Because the murder charges stemmed from a death that occurred so long ago, the law that had been in effect in 1978 would apply to the case rather than contemporary law.

While Krajcir was assigned a public defender in Illinois and still awaited charges for killing Witte in Marion, authorities in Pennsylvania intended to avoid the whole mess by keeping the inmate where he was. They planned to convict him by video, so he'd never have to leave his secure facility in Illinois. A Pennsylvania state cop served Krajcir the arrest warrant, but the rest of the process they intended to handle without any face-to-face contact. Krajcir could plead by way of closed-circuit video if he and his attorney agreed to do it that way. Berks County, Pennsylvania district attorney John Adams was all for getting the job done and avoiding the messy extradition process altogether.

Krajcir pleaded guilty in Williamson County to killing Virginia Lee Witte and received a forty-year sentence—that's forty more years in addition to the forty he'd have to serve for the Sheppard killing.

But as Missouri authorities, awaiting extradition of the now convicted killer, made plans to house Krajcir, something else was going on with the Illinois inmate.

Echols and Smith had scoured the records of dozens of unsolved rapes, murders, and burglaries, looking for those that fit Krajcir's profile, the pattern they'd become so familiar with. They kept returning to several they'd been unable to locate: the two rapes and the stabbing in Mount Vernon, crimes to which Krajcir confessed, but they could find no account of the assaults.

When Mount Vernon couldn't find any police reports of the crimes either, Echols began releasing some of the details Krajcir had given to him and Smith to local news media, hoping someone would recognize the accounts. It worked. A television reporter for the local KFVS12 began digging in the local library, and found a decades-old news brief recounting Grover Thompson's conviction for the assault on Ida White that duplicated the assault Krajcir claimed to have committed.

The reporter contacted Stephen Swofford, Grover Thompson's original public defender, and informed him of the charges. As far as Swofford was concerned, Krajcir's confessions only confirmed what he'd known all along, that his client had been absolutely innocent.

The news that Thompson had been wrongly convicted, and had died in prison years before the truth came out, set off a firestorm of controversy. Detectives Echols, Smith, and others who worked on the Virginia Lee Witte, Joyce Tharp, and Myrtle Rupp homicides felt certain that Krajcir was telling the the truth. Mount Vernon officials insisted that the right man had been convicted for stabbing Ida White. The current Mount Vernon police chief suggested that the confession was phony and should cast serious doubt on Krajcir's credibility. He learned that both Grover Thompson and Timothy Krajcir had once been housed in the same prison, and he was confident that they had, at some point, discussed the facts of the case.

Mount Vernon refused to reconsider the stabbing case, but they did send a detective down to Tamms to interview Krajcir about the sexual assaults. Krajcir later said he thought that the detective hadn't believed anything he had to say.

By this point in time, so many court dates had been made and later scrapped that Swingle decided to put off Krajcir's initial appearance in Missouri until the man was physically sitting in the county jail.

Krajcir ultimately faced thirteen felony charges in Cape Girardeau. The five added charges had come only a few weeks earlier. Swingle had consulted with Carol Kirchner, Dorothy Quay, and Gretchen Lockwood, the three women whom Krajcir had assaulted while their children were in Kirchner's home, as well as Eunice Seabaugh and Grace Larkin. They all decided to pursue criminal charges.

Krajcir's initial hearing was handled by a jail cam, a closed-circuit video that sends images to the courtroom without the defendant having to leave his jail cell, but he needed to be present in the courtroom for the plea hearing. He would step into a Missouri courtroom for the first time to face the families of his victims, the citizens, and a judge.

Because of the sheer number of people Swingle expected to attend the hearing, he requested that it be held at the federal building in Cape Girardeau. The building had better security than the county courthouse, in case someone wanted to act on one of the death threats made against the defendant. Timothy Krajcir had done a lot of horrible things in this town, to this town, and authorities didn't want to take a chance on some nut trying to make a name for himself. Swingle actually changed the date so the federal courthouse would be available.

Most of the original detectives who had worked on the cases were undecided about whether they wanted to attend the hearing. Margie Call's granddaughter, Le Call, a model, wanted to be there, but she had a photo shoot in Paris on the newly scheduled date, and she sent Swingle a scathing letter for changing it. It was the only time the prosecutor ever received an angry letter from a supermodel.

Margie's son Don Call's recurring dream had changed. Knowing of Krajcir's basketball prowess, the ex–college basketball star, now dreamed several times in the weeks leading up to the trial that he had the chance to go one-on-one with the convict. If Don won, Krajcir would face the death penalty for the murder.

Why had Krajcir done it? This question had plagued him for years. But on April 4, when Krajcir opened his mouth and spoke for the first time in a public setting about his crimes, Don still didn't get an answer. Krajcir described each crime, making sure the people sitting in the courtroom recognized that their loved ones hadn't done anything to incur his wrath, but even he couldn't explain why he'd killed them.

After this, Grace Larkin stood up. She spoke about how difficult it had been for her to attend the legal proceedings. She looked at Krajcir as she bravely pushed forward, saying that he'd put a cloud over her head that she'd never been able to lift until today. She'd prayed to God that her children wouldn't remember seeing her assault, but her son remembered the day so clearly she'd had to ask detectives not to interview him. She feared his rage would be too great if he were asked to speak of what he'd witnessed. After twenty-six years of living with the fear, and the pain, though, today felt different to Grace. It felt like a holiday of some kind.

Krajcir listened to every victim's relative get up and speak. Don Call spoke of how his mother had been robbed of the chance to see her beautiful grandchildren.

The judge who presided over the hearing happened to be Cape Girardeau County circuit judge Benjamin Lewis, who had grown up in Cape Girardeau. Like everyone else present, the grisly murders had had an impact on his life. Sheila Cole had been in the same sorority as his wife. Their sorority pledge class had been little sisters to his own fraternity chapter. And of course, like so many others in the courtroom, he had known Brenda Parsh.

Krajcir mumbled that he'd like the opportunity to speak, and he was granted it, though when he turned to face the families, Lewis admonished him, telling him to face the bench. Tears began falling beneath the thick black rubber frames of Krajcir's glasses.

He said he wanted the families to know he'd heard every word they'd said.

"I'm terribly sorry for what I've done," he said. He vowed to spend the rest of his days trying to help others like him from traveling down the same path, crediting sex offender programs with being successful at keeping men like him off the streets.

Judge Lewis let Krajcir finish before handing down a sentence of fifty years per charge. Krajcir would have to serve a minimum of 650 years in prison before parole. The apology had taken Lewis by surprise, he said, and he wanted the man before him to live the remainder of his life fully aware of the pain he'd caused.

"I hope you never take another breath as a free man," the judge said.

Two months later, another life sentence was added to Krajcir's string when he was convicted by video in Pennsylvania for the murder of Myrtle Rupp. Rupp's nephew said he hoped the man got killed in prison.

At the time of this book's publication, Krajcir had yet to be tried for Joyce Tharp's murder in Kentucky, and Grover Thompson's conviction for attacking Ida White in Mount Vernon was still standing. Some of Thompson's relatives had talked about contacting an attorney, wishing to clear his name even if it was too late to free him literally. A lawyer near Chicago offered to comb through the transcripts from Grover's trial, but the case seems to have stalled. To prove a wrongful conviction case in a civil litigation is difficult because one must not only prove actual innocence but willful misconduct or malice on the part of police or prosecution.

Krajcir was put in isolation in the county jail. To the sheriff's best recollection, the jail had never before housed a serial killer. Deputies said the older man was the ideal prisoner, quiet and undemanding. His only request had been that he be allowed to watch the NCAA playoffs in men's basketball. He was a rabid North Carolina fan. Guards put a small TV in his cell.

The same week that his team lost in the finals, Krajcir received thirteen life sentences for the crimes he'd committed in Cape Girardeau. Thirty years, one for each felony, was the equivalent of a life sentence. There were still other crimes he had to account for, but hearing him receive hundreds of years in prison without the possibility of parole had the ring of finality. Krajcir's tears provided a sense of closure as well. The town on which he'd preyed for five years finally got the chance to make him regret what he'd done to its citizens. The reign of terror had come to an end.

Epilogue

Timothy Krajcir said he was sorry.

Maybe he truly was. But not everyone believed his apology. After the hearing, Grace Larkin said she didn't believe him. Standing in the foyer of the sprawling federal building, I didn't know if I bought it either. I thought back to the interview I'd done a few short weeks earlier, in the visiting room of the Cape Girardeau County Jail.

Krajcir's arrogance had been unrelenting. Though he'd spoken quietly, courteously, and with intelligence, his inflated sense of self overwhelmed everyone in the room.

That was the Krajcir I could easily see killing nine women and raping countless others. The one who laid in wait for his victims, choosing them on no basis other than their vulnerability. The man who eluded police for nearly three decades by avoiding any ties to his victims, planning his hunting expeditions carefully. The college student who majored in criminal justice and psychology. The inmate who convinced every prison official who oversaw his care that he was a model prisoner, a safe candidate for release back into society.

Echols had been right. There *were* two Tims. One was an educated, polite, respected citizen who charmed co-workers, friends, even psychiatrists; the Tim who cooperated with police and was responsive to their questions; the Tim who cried for his victims in the courtroom, weeping for the time he'd stolen from them and their loved ones. And then there was the Tim who preyed on women in the Heartland without a shred of guilt, walking the streets as a free man, raping and killing whenever the mood seemed to strike him. The man who pulled a blue bandanna over his face and became a monster.

Bridget DiCosmo is an award-winning crime reporter for the *Southeast Missourian*, a daily newspaper in Cape Girardeau, Missouri. She pursued a graduate education at Point Park University in Pittsburgh, Pennsylvania, and holds an undergraduate degree in history from St. John's University in Queens, New York.

When she is not digging into the world of crime, Bridget relaxes by riding horses and spending time at home with Bandit, her King Charles spaniel, and Natalie, her cat.